48 Great Scroll Saw Projects

Patrick Spielman & Rick Longabaugh

Acknowledgements & Credits

Patrick Spielman
Rick and Karen Longabaugh
Lorna Smith Graphic Design
Owen & Owen Photography

Contents

Introduction

This book features over 40 beautiful and functional projects for the scroll sawing enthusiast. Many offer a choice of three different design motifs; Country, Victorian or Southwest themes, simply by selecting from interchangeable patterns of decorative components. These projects are new design innovations incorporating the combination of thick (3/4") and thin (1/4" - 3/8") materials.

Many projects require some very basic routing operations. Edges that are fully or partially rounded over add a professional touch and increased visual interest. If you don't own a router or care to do the routing work yourself you may want to solicit the help of a woodworking friend. The amount of routing necessary to make these projects is actually very minimal.

A brief introductory chapter provides basic techniques and tips to help you get started. If scroll sawing and routing are new to you, we recommend the book, SCROLL SAW BASICS and ROUTER BASICS, both published by Sterling Publishing Co., New York, NY.

Several of the projects require some basic bevel sawing techniques. Sawing certain parts with the saw table tilted slightly allows you to make some very interesting projects. One type sure to be a favorite is the 3-dimensional collapsible basket projects with folding supports and bases. These unusual projects are cut from a single, flat board. Other bevel sawing projects involve a special technique of cutting out decorative elements that become raised in relief above a flat background. These innovative and trend setting designs are certain to be very popular as well.

Projects incorporating simple "fit-up" and pendulum clock inserts will be well received as gifts to the home or they can be produced to sell. In fact, every project was carefully designed to exhibit good market appeal with high potential for selling at craft shows, gift shops or bazaars. In addition to a variety of clocks and folding baskets, you will find decorative projects for Christmas plus beautiful shelves, frames, a hand mirror, tissue box, jewelry rack, and many more items that are not only useful and beautiful to look at but also great fun to make.

Basic Tips and Techniques

Copying and Transferring Patterns

The quickest and currently the most widely employed process of transfering patterns to the wood simply requires making a photo copy of the pattern and then adhering it to your wood with a temporary bonding spray adhesive. If you don't own or have access to a photo copy machine, visit your public library or check the yellow pages for copying shops near you.

Be sure to use the *temporary bonding* type of spray adhesive. That is, one that allows you to easily remove (peel) the pattern from the wood when all sawing is completed. One of the best brands we've used is 3-M's Scotch Brand Spray Mount Adhesive. Such adhesives are available in craft stores and from mail order sources. Just scissor cut your paper pattern copy to a rough size and spray a very light mist to the back of the pattern only, wait 10 to 30 seconds and hand press it onto the wood. Note: be sure to spray the adhesive in a well ventilated area.

Do not spray adhesive directly onto the wood itself. First time users should test the technique with scrap wood to get a feel for the best amount of adhesive coverage. Unexpectedly, very little adhesive is required. See Illus. 1.

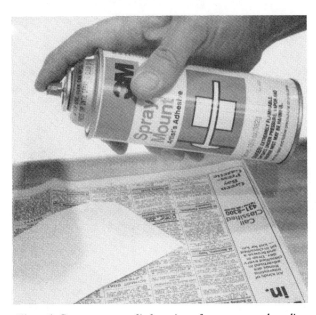

Illus. 1 Spray a very light mist of temporary bonding adhesive on the back of a photo copied paper pattern. Note the newspaper catching the overspray.

Duplicate or Stack Sawing

When two or more identical parts are needed, cut them all at once stacked one on top of another. The layers can be held together in various ways but the easiest method is to tack them together. Use small wire nails or brads driven into the waste areas. See Illus. 2-4. Tip: Sometimes you may want to use a waste back-up as a bottom layer to minimize or eliminate feathering or tear out that occurs as the blade exits through the bottom surface of the work piece. New reverse teeth blades that have lower teeth designed to cut on the upstroke greatly minimize tearout problems. Reverse teeth blades are the recommended choice of professionals.

Illus. 2 Stack cut when two or more identical parts are required as for this napkin/ letter holder project. Here, two layers are tacked together with small wire nails.

Veining

Veining is a simple technique that brings a "life-like" appearance to many projects. For instance, the folds of clothing or the veins of a leaf take on a more realistic appearance when this technique is incorporated. To vein, simply saw all black lines as indicated on the pattern. Some areas you will be able to vein by simply sawing inward from an outside edge, while to vein other areas you will need to drill a tiny blade entry hole, and then proceed to saw.

Silhouette Backing

Many of the projects cut from thin material can easily have a contrasting background added, which beautifully enhances the appearance of the design. This background

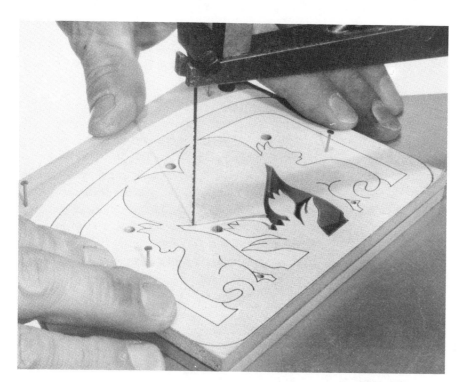

Illus. 3 Sawing two parts for the letter/napkin holder project at the same time.

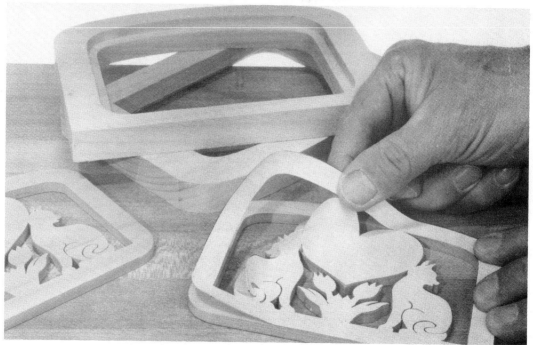

Illus. 4 After sawing, the pattern should remove easily.

offers versatility - it can be made from hardwood or plywood and it can be stained, painted, or even left natural.

To utilize this technique, first saw the fretwork portion of the project, leaving the outer shape uncut until you are ready to glue on the backing. Use a painting or cosmetic sponge to apply a thin layer of glue to the backside of the fretted workpiece. Center this onto the backing blank and clamp until dry. Then simply cut along the outside line where indicated and use a 1/4" R roundover bit if desired. Sand where necessary.

Routing and Drilling

Basic routing and drilling operations are required for many of the projects. The two primary routing jobs are rounding over edges and cutting rabbets to receive thin, fretted panels. We recommend considering the new European safety bits when purchasing new or replacement router bits. See Illus. 5 and 6. Most routing can be done with a portable hand held router as shown in Illus. 7. This is slightly tricky. Some of the project parts may be fairly

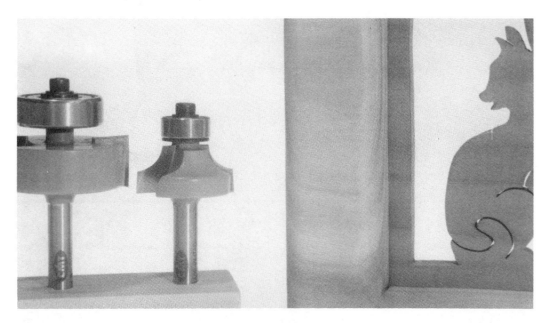

Illus. 5 Many projects require routing operations. Most can be completed using the two bits shown here. Left to right: a 1/4" rabbeting bit and a 1/4" radius roundover bit. Note: These are the new, full body European style safety bits that minimize the potential for dangerous kickback.

Illus. 6 Typical rabbeting and roundover routing cuts shown on parts for the napkin/letter holder project.

small which can be difficult to clamp and the router tends to be tippy when doing such work. Always wear eye protection for all routing jobs.

Routing with a router table is easier provided all of the necessary safety precautions are entertained. Use safety style bits, feed against the bit rotation (Illus. 8 and 9), and be sure to protect your fingers, keeping them well away from the cutting area. Use pusher blocks with rubberized pads that effectively grip and control the work piece during feeding.

Drilling and countersinking operations for screw holes is pretty much a standard procedure that can be done with an electric hand drill or a drill press as appropriate. ***Important:*** Sometimes it may be best to drill after routing

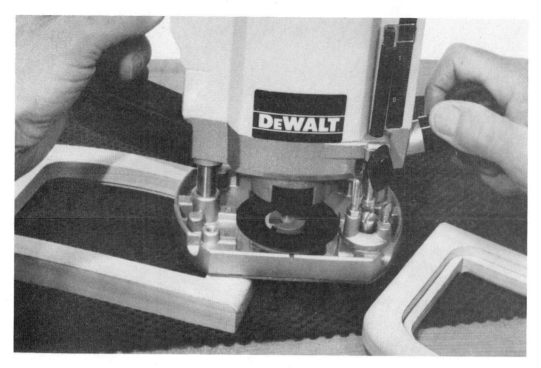

Illus. 7 Hand-held routing with the work held firm, without clamps on a non-slip friction pad.

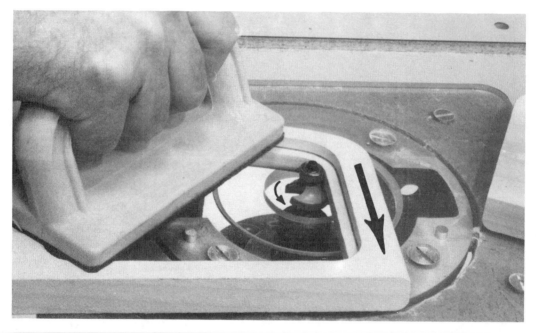

Illus. 8 Rounding over and rabbeting an inside edge on the router table. Notice the use of a push block for maximum safety and that the workpiece is fed against the bit's rotation.

and sometimes it's best to drill before routing. Whenever a hole is made into an edge where the bearing or pilot of a router bit must bear against it, be sure that the size or location of the hole will not detour the desired course of the bit. Thus, you may want to drill a small hole first, rout the edge next, and make a larger or countersink hole last.

The photos (Illus. 10, 11, and 12) show a useful drilling jig which makes easy work of centering holes in the edges of work pieces. Once made, it will have many uses in the average shop. You can make it accommodate stock of various thickness by either shimming under the workpiece or under the drill itself.

Sanding and Finishing

Generally, it's best to sand all flat surfaces smooth before adhering the patterns to the workpiece. Properly routed

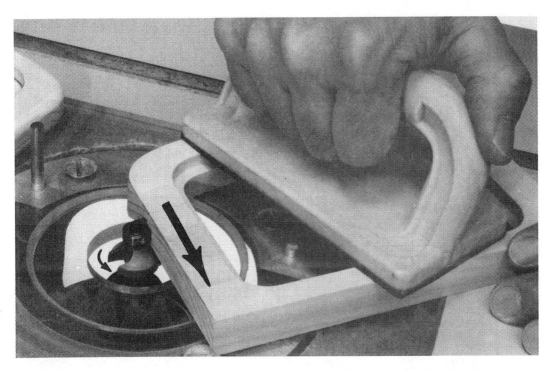

Illust. 9 Rounding over an outside edge on the router table. A push block safely feeds the workpiece against the rotational direction of the bit.

Illus. 10 This drilling jig makes perfectly centered holes in the edges of workpieces. Change shim panels as necessary to accommodate different stock thicknesses.

and scroll sawn surfaces should require very little sanding if at all. One sanding system we've found very useful to sand routed edges and to remove feathering and soften fret cuts is the flutter sanding accessory for the hand drill or drill press. Special individual cut flutter sheets, are stack mounted on an arbor and used as shown in Illus. 13. A package of 50 sheets, available in various grits, with an arbor is very reasonable. Contact the Klingspore Sanding Catalog, P.O. Box 3737, Hickory, N.C. 28603 or phone 1-800-228-0000.

The method we utilize and recommend for finishing is essentially a dipping process with a penetrating oil finish. Use any of the major brands of penetrating oil finishes and a shallow pan as shown in the photos (Illus. 14 and 15). If you are already employing a different finishing system effectively, by all means continue. Just as they say, "There's more than one way to skin a cat"; there are various approaches to almost every aspect of woodworking. Always employ those processes that are most appropriate for your individual needs and expectations.

Illus. 11 A small piece of tape on the bit indicates the hole depth.

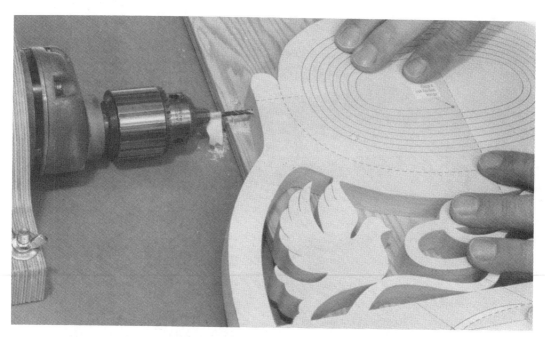

Illus. 12 Drilling pivot points for a collapsible basket with the aid of the jig.
The work is fed into the rotating bit.

Illus. 13 Using a flutter wheel to soften sharp edges and to remove feathering which may occur on the exit side of the cut.

Illus. 14 This dip method of finishing fretwork using a shallow tray as shown is the quickest and easiest technique.

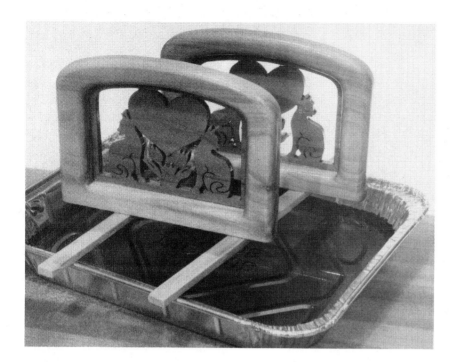

Bevel Sawing-Projects & Techniques

As noted earlier, some special projects require certain cuts to be made with the scroll saw table slightly tilted. This is known as bevel sawing. Bevel sawing is employed in the process of raising designated cut out project areas in relief from the surrounding background. The large wall shelf pages 33-39 and the wall sconce projects pages 30-32 incorporate these techniques and design elements.

Likewise, bevel sawing is employed to make the continuous spiral bevel cuts necessary to make the planter basket project pages 51-56 and three other collapsible basket projects beginning on page 43. See the drawings (Illus. 16 and 17).

There are two factors that determine how far a cut out can be raised in relief and how deep a spiral cut basket will drop open. These factors are: (1) the cutting width of the blade (kerf size) and (2) the amount of table tilt specified in degrees. In general, the wider the blade's cutting path (kerf), the more table tilt required. Or, remember that the more vertical the cut, the more the part can be raised and the further a spiral cut will drop open creating a deeper basket cavity. See the drawing, (Illus. 17)

Usually it's best to use a No. 5 or No. 7 blade for all profile and decorative internal sawing. Use a No. 9 blade to cut the continuous spiral basket rungs. Since there are differences in blades from one manufacturer to another, and table tilt scales are not always accurate, it's always best to make some test cuts. Use scrap of the same thickness and species selected for your project. The blade sizes and table tilt angles suggested on the pattern drawings for bevel cuts are just that - - suggestive. You will need to determine your own specifications based upon the cutting characteristics of your own blades and your own scroll saw. See the photos (Illus. 18 and 19).

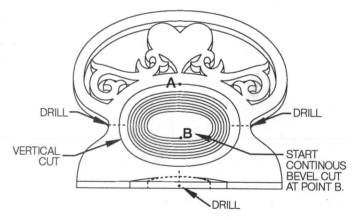

Illus. 16 Typical basket shows locations for pivot screws and blade threading hole locations for making internal cuts.

Making Baskets

Illus. 17 Comparative bevel cuts determining how far a basket will drop open. Left: Basket cavity is too shallow (caused by too much table tilt). Right: Just the right cut at a lesser angle and less table tilt than the basket at the left.

The basic procedure for making the collapsible basket components of the projects on the forgoing pages is as follows:

Step 1. After the outside profile has been cut out, mark the holes for the screw pivots with a scratch awl.

Step 2. Drill the specified size to a depth as specified by the length of the dashed lines given on the pattern. See the drawing (Illus. 16) Refer to pages 8-10 for an easy to make jig that converts your portable hand drill into a horizontal drilling device.

Step 3. To cut the basket component free, drill a small blade entry hole at point "A" in the drawing (Illus. 16). Note: This is a vertical cut with the table set square to the blade.

Step 4. To make the basket's continuous bevel cut, drill a small blade entry hole at point "B" of the drawing (Illus. 16). Tilt your table down to the left. Saw, following the solid spiral line to its end. Note: If your table only tilts down to the right, you will need to turn your basket over when you've completed cutting the rungs for it to open properly.

Step 5. Round over the top edge(s) of the basket and other edges as may be designated on the pattern. Carefully sand the surfaces with a flutter wheel sander to remove any feathering and to slightly soften the sharp edges.

Step 6. Finish by dipping into a penetrating oil and then assemble the component parts. Test all pivoting connections and the basket's collapsing action.

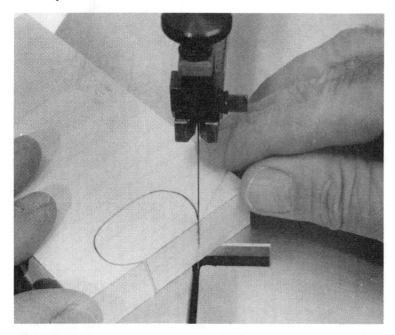

Illus. 18 Making a test bevel cut (in this nearly full oval or circular shape) to check the appropriate table tilt adjustment for the blade being used.

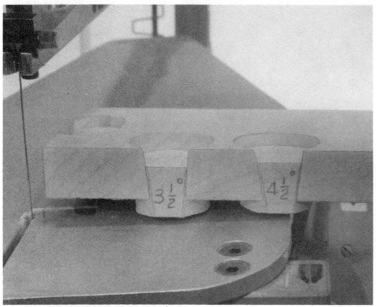

Illus. 19 Note that the greater the blade tilt, the less the cut part can move vertically before being wedged tightly against the sides of the cut. Sawing at lesser angles (more vertical), increases the vertical movement of the cut piece or the deeper cavity a collapsible basket will have.

NATIVITY SCENE

STOCK: 1/4" - 3/8"
HARDWOOD OR
PLYWOOD

CENTER 3/4" -
1 1/2" HINGES
WHERE
INDICATED

14

NATIVITY SCENE

CENTER 3/4" -
1 1/2" HINGES
WHERE
INDICATED

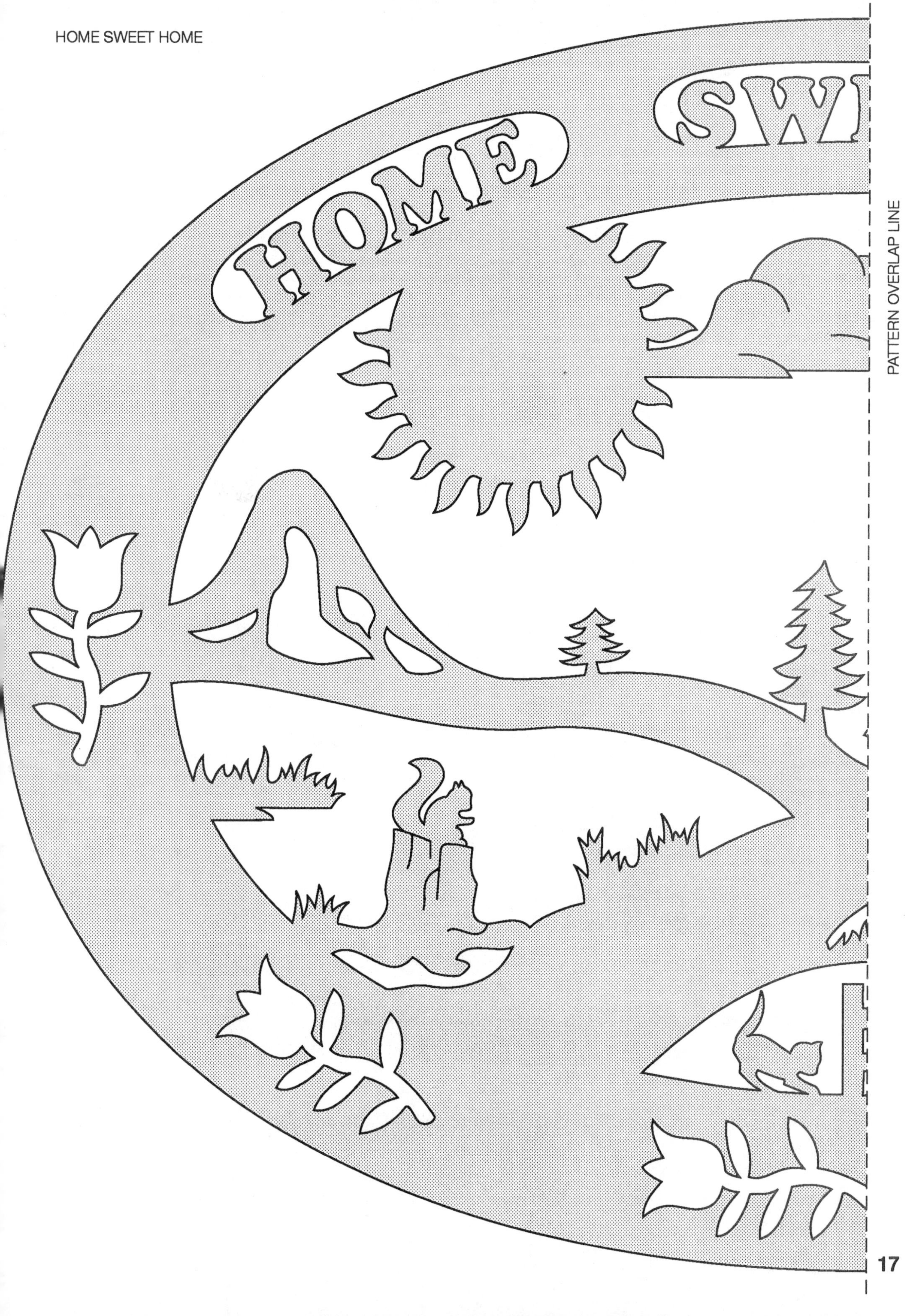
HOME
SW
PATTERN OVERLAP LINE

HOME SWEET HOME

STOCK: 1/4" - 3/8"
HARDWOOD OR
PLYWOOD

VICTORIAN HAND MIRROR

STOCK: 1/4" - 3/8"
HARDWOOD OR PLYWOOD

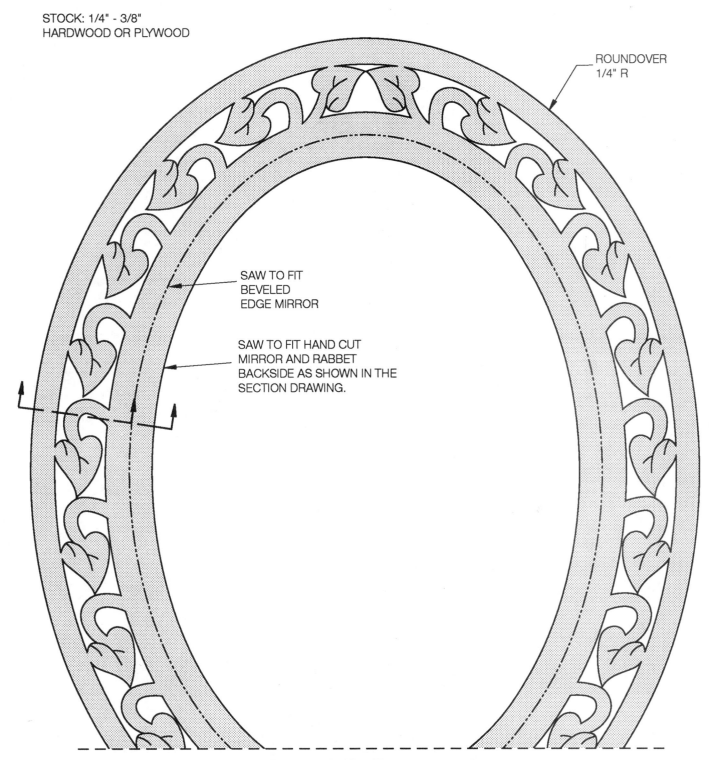

ROUNDOVER
1/4" R

SAW TO FIT
BEVELED
EDGE MIRROR

SAW TO FIT HAND CUT
MIRROR AND RABBET
BACKSIDE AS SHOWN IN THE
SECTION DRAWING.

PATTERN OVERLAP LINE

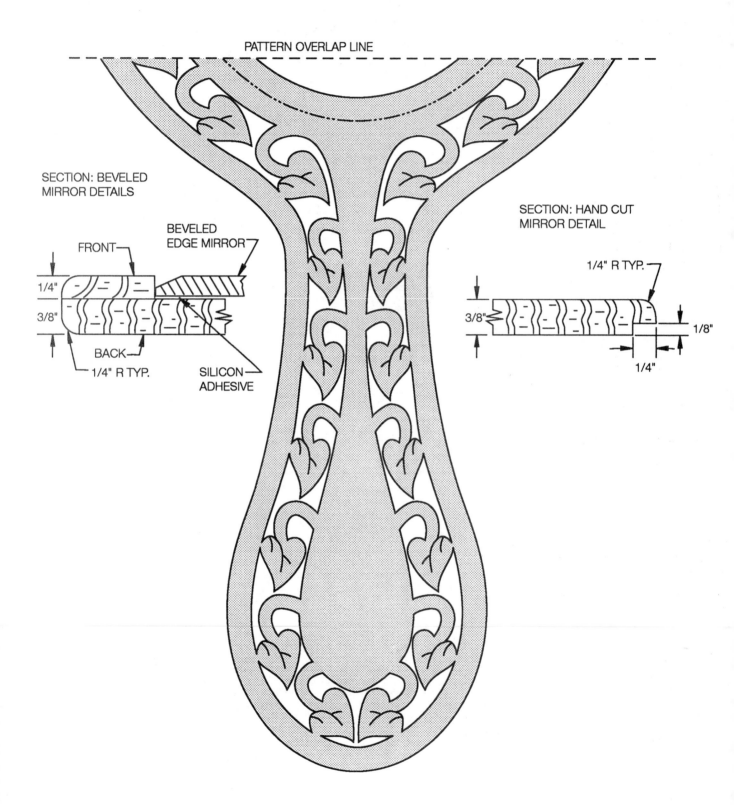

PATTERN OVERLAP LINE

SECTION: BEVELED
MIRROR DETAILS

FRONT

BEVELED
EDGE MIRROR

1/4"

3/8"

BACK

1/4" R TYP.

SILICON
ADHESIVE

SECTION: HAND CUT
MIRROR DETAIL

1/4" R TYP.

3/8"

1/8"

1/4"

NECKLACE/
KEY RACK

STOCK: 1/4" - 3/8"
HARDWOOD OR
PLYWOOD

NECKLACE/
KEY RACK

PATTERN OVERLAP LINE

DRILL TO INSERT
WOODEN PEGS OR
DOWELS

VICTORIAN MIRROR / PICTURE FRAME

STOCK: 1/4" - 3/8" HARDWOOD OR PLYWOOD

SAW TO FIT
BEVELED
EDGE MIRROR

SECTION: BEVELED
MIRROR DETAILS

BEVELED
EDGE MIRROR

FRONT

1/4"

3/8"

BACK

1/4" R TYP.

SILICON
ADHESIVE

ROUNDOVER EDGE, 1/4" R

PATTERN OVERLAP LINE

SAW TO FIT HAND CUT
MIRROR AND RABBET
BACKSIDE AS SHOWN IN
THE SECTION DRAWING

SECTION: HAND CUT
MIRROR DETAIL

1/4" R TYP.

3/8"

1/8"

1/4"

PATTERN OVERLAP LINE

VICTORIAN CROSS
WITH SHELF

27

VICTORIAN CROSS
WITH SHELF

STOCK: 1/4" HARDWOOD
OR PLYWOOD

PATTERN OVERLAP LINE

28

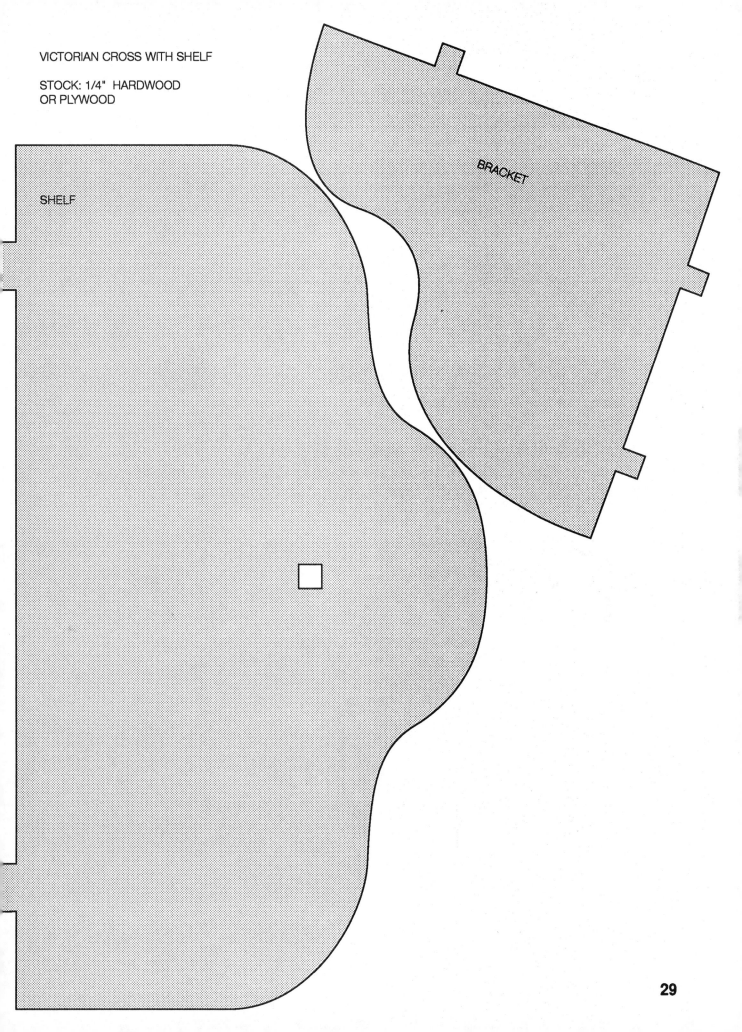

VICTORIAN CROSS WITH SHELF

STOCK: 1/4" HARDWOOD
OR PLYWOOD

SHELF

BRACKET

VICTORIAN SCONCE

STOCK: 3/4" HARDWOOD

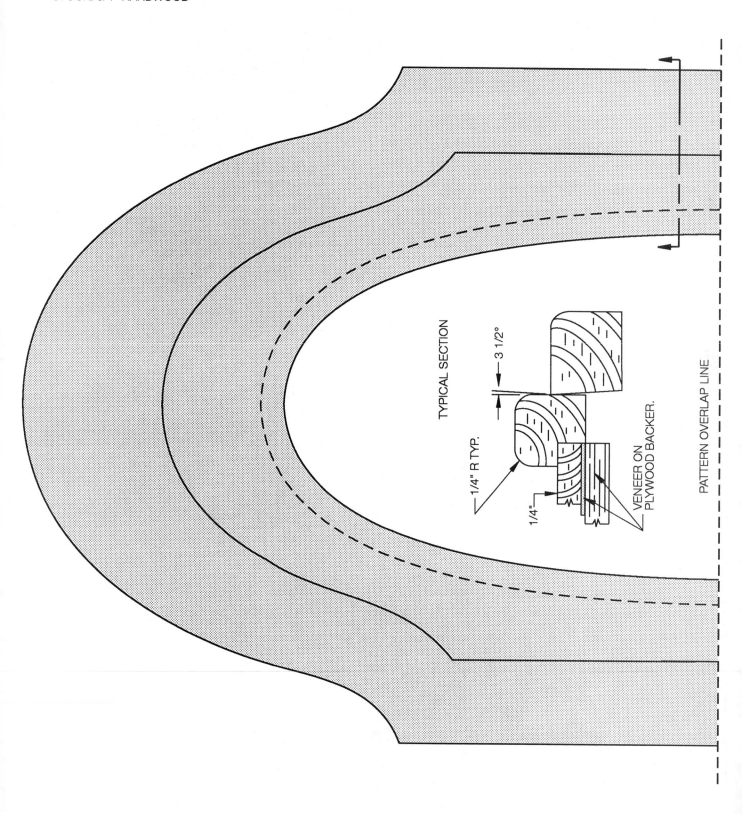

TYPICAL SECTION

3 1/2°

1/4" R TYP.

1/4"

VENEER ON PLYWOOD BACKER.

PATTERN OVERLAP LINE

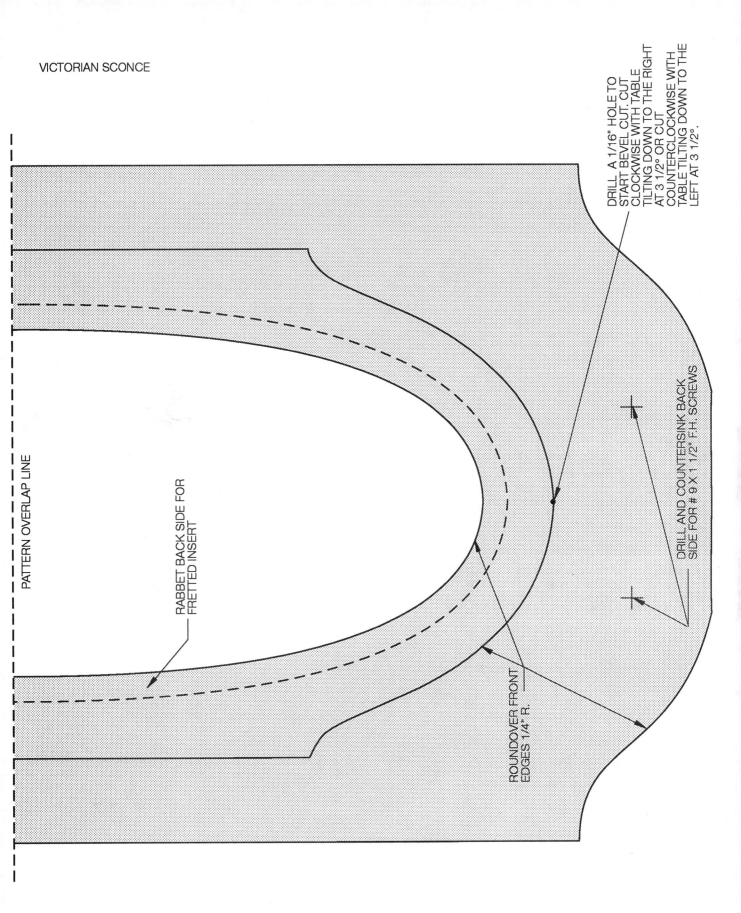

DRILL A 1/16" HOLE TO
START BEVEL CUT. CUT
CLOCKWISE WITH TABLE
TILTING DOWN TO THE RIGHT
AT 3 1/2° OR CUT
COUNTERCLOCKWISE WITH
TABLE TILTING DOWN TO THE
LEFT AT 3 1/2°.

DRILL AND COUNTERSINK BACK
SIDE FOR # 9 X 1 1/2" F.H. SCREWS

PATTERN OVERLAP LINE

RABBET BACK SIDE FOR
FRETTED INSERT

ROUNDOVER FRONT
EDGES 1/4" R.

31

VICTORIAN SCONCE

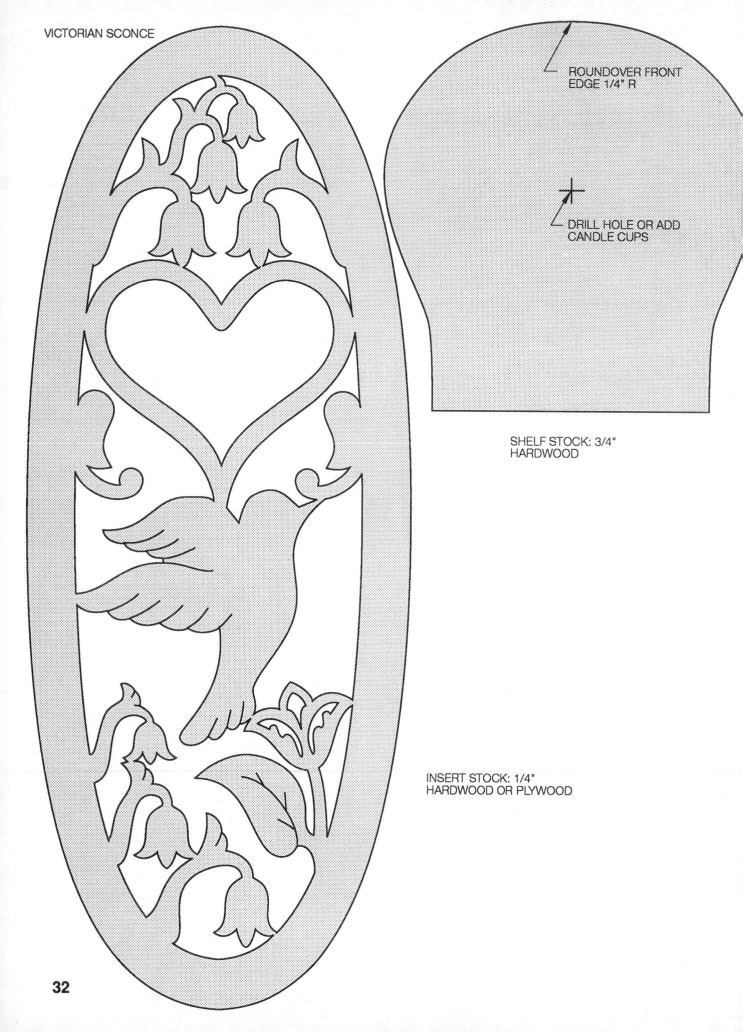

ROUNDOVER FRONT
EDGE 1/4" R

DRILL HOLE OR ADD
CANDLE CUPS

SHELF STOCK: 3/4"
HARDWOOD

INSERT STOCK: 1/4"
HARDWOOD OR PLYWOOD

LARGE SHELF

STOCK: 3/4" HARDWOOD

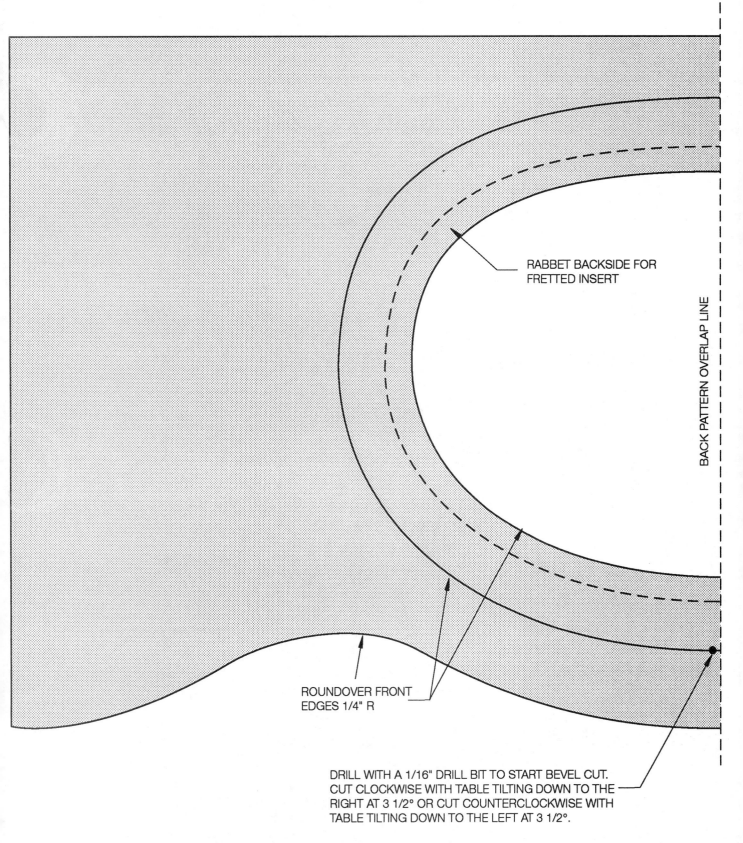

RABBET BACKSIDE FOR
FRETTED INSERT

BACK PATTERN OVERLAP LINE

ROUNDOVER FRONT
EDGES 1/4" R

DRILL WITH A 1/16" DRILL BIT TO START BEVEL CUT.
CUT CLOCKWISE WITH TABLE TILTING DOWN TO THE
RIGHT AT 3 1/2° OR CUT COUNTERCLOCKWISE WITH
TABLE TILTING DOWN TO THE LEFT AT 3 1/2°.

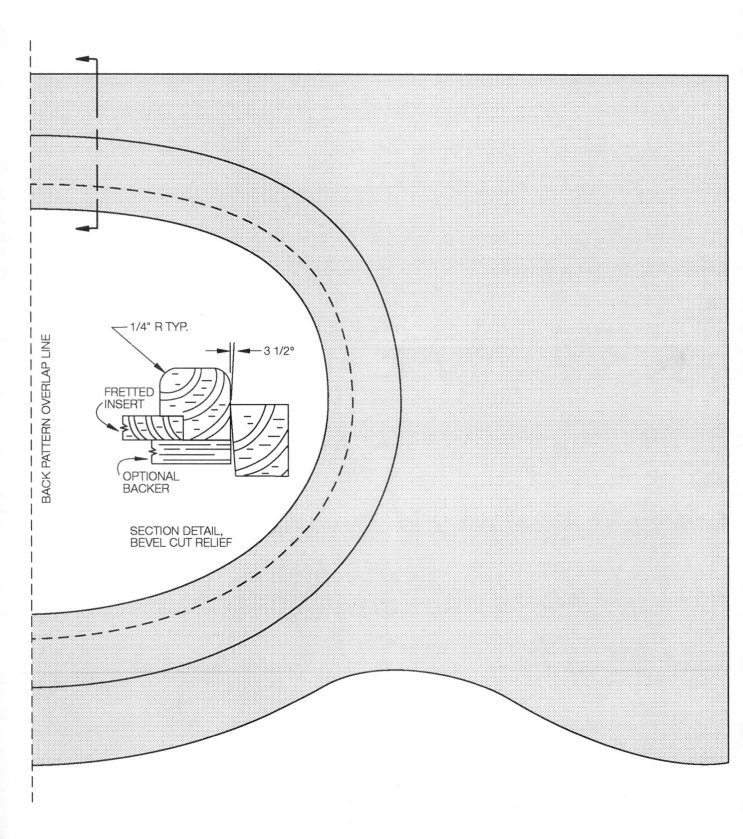

1/4" R TYP.

3 1/2°

FRETTED
INSERT

OPTIONAL
BACKER

SECTION DETAIL,
BEVEL CUT RELIEF

BACK PATTERN OVERLAP LINE

LARGE SHELF

INSERT STOCK: 1/4"
HARDWOOD OR PLYWOOD

LARGE SHELF

NOTE: OPTIONAL - CUT
       ANOTHER BLANK
       BACKING OF
       CONTRASTING
       MATERIAL FOR
       VISUAL EFFECT AS
       DESIRED.

STOCK: 1/4" HARDWOOD
OR PLYWOOD

LARGE SHELF

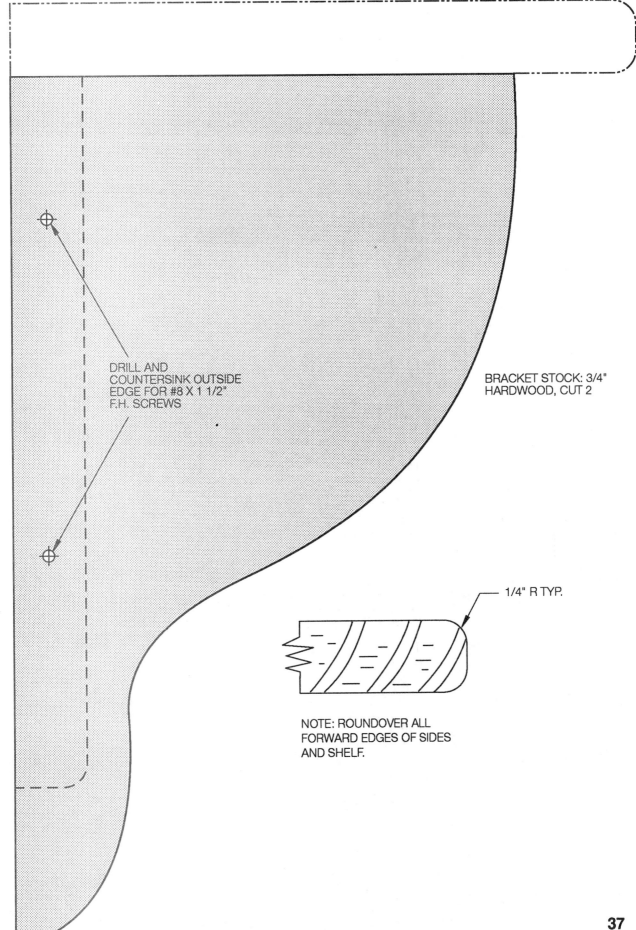

DRILL AND
COUNTERSINK OUTSIDE
EDGE FOR #8 X 1 1/2"
F.H. SCREWS

BRACKET STOCK: 3/4"
HARDWOOD, CUT 2

1/4" R TYP.

NOTE: ROUNDOVER ALL
FORWARD EDGES OF SIDES
AND SHELF.

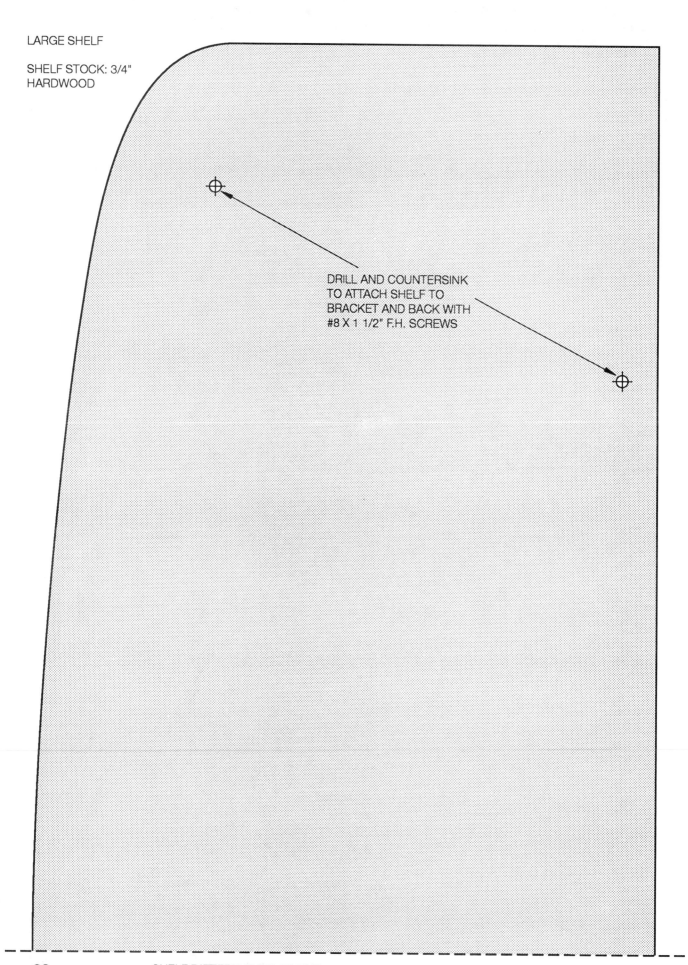

LARGE SHELF

SHELF STOCK: 3/4"
HARDWOOD

DRILL AND COUNTERSINK
TO ATTACH SHELF TO
BRACKET AND BACK WITH
#8 X 1 1/2" F.H. SCREWS

38   SHELF PATTERN OVERLAP LINE

SHELF PATTERN OVERLAP LINE

EARRING HOLDER

STOCK: 3/4" HARDWOOD

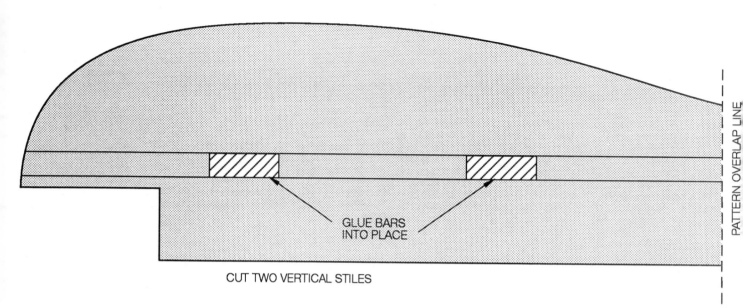

GLUE BARS
INTO PLACE

CUT TWO VERTICAL STILES

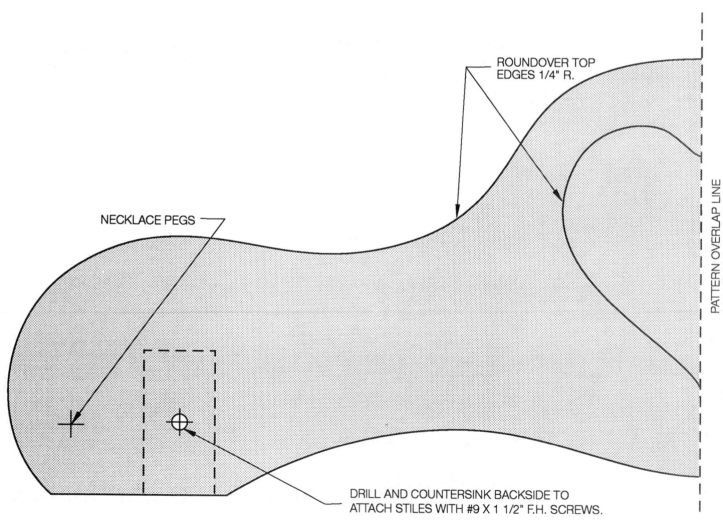

ROUNDOVER TOP
EDGES 1/4" R.

NECKLACE PEGS

DRILL AND COUNTERSINK BACKSIDE TO
ATTACH STILES WITH #9 X 1 1/2" F.H. SCREWS.

PATTERN OVERLAP LINE

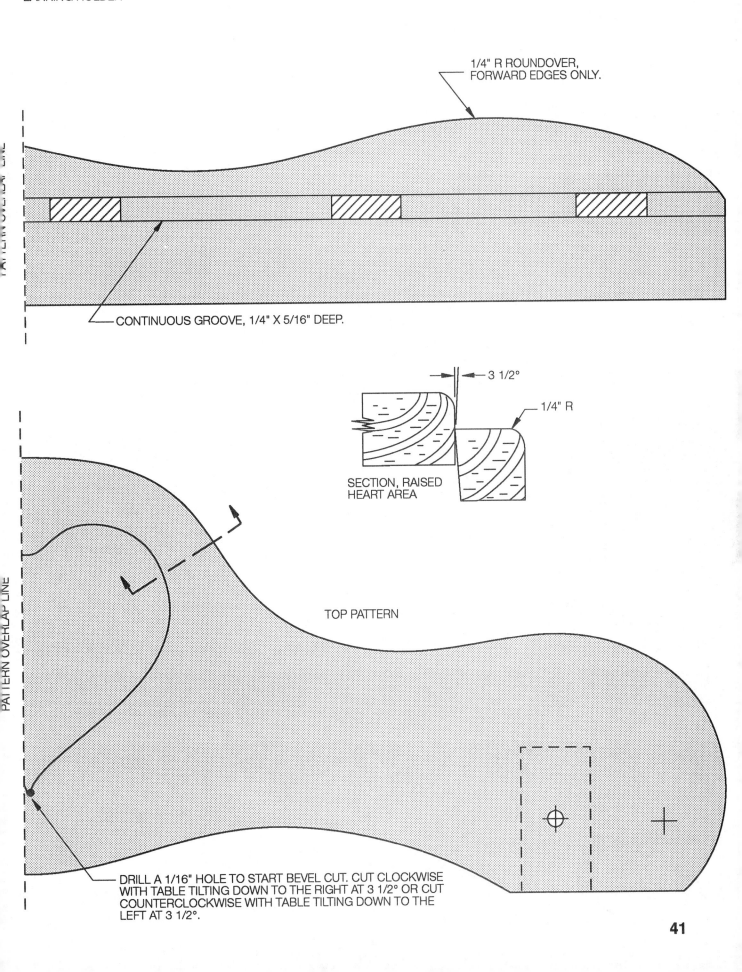

1/4" R ROUNDOVER, FORWARD EDGES ONLY.

CONTINUOUS GROOVE, 1/4" X 5/16" DEEP.

3 1/2°

1/4" R

SECTION, RAISED HEART AREA

TOP PATTERN

PATTERN OVERLAP LINE

DRILL A 1/16" HOLE TO START BEVEL CUT. CUT CLOCKWISE WITH TABLE TILTING DOWN TO THE RIGHT AT 3 1/2° OR CUT COUNTERCLOCKWISE WITH TABLE TILTING DOWN TO THE LEFT AT 3 1/2°.

41

EARRING HOLDER

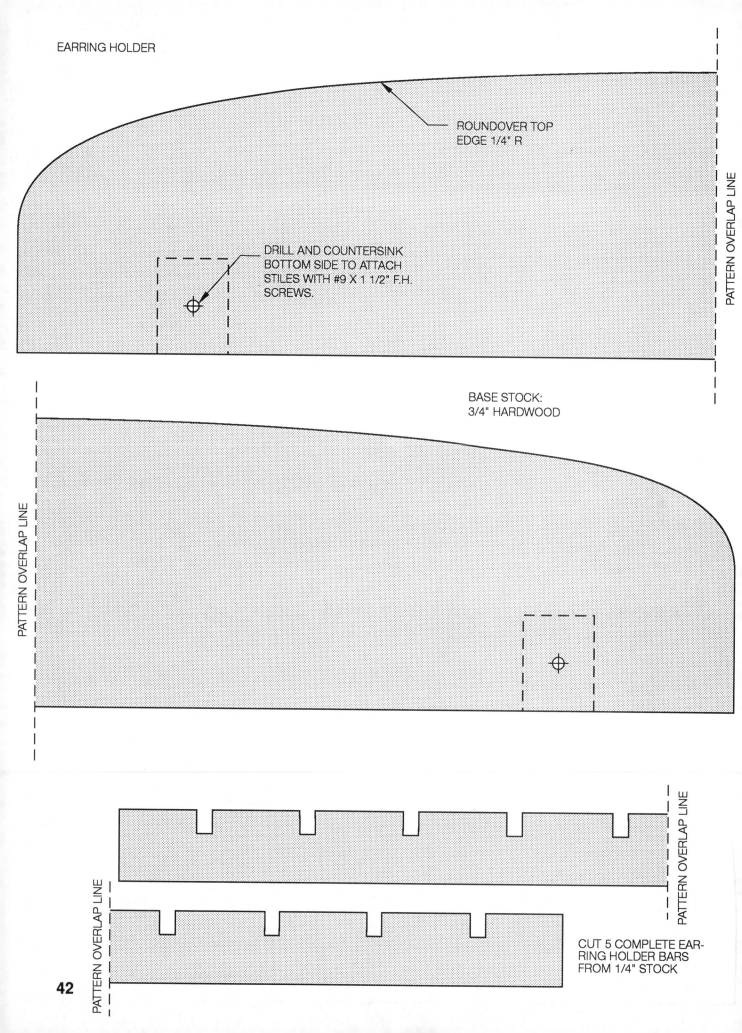

ROUNDOVER TOP
EDGE 1/4" R

DRILL AND COUNTERSINK
BOTTOM SIDE TO ATTACH
STILES WITH #9 X 1 1/2" F.H.
SCREWS.

BASE STOCK:
3/4" HARDWOOD

PATTERN OVERLAP LINE

PATTERN OVERLAP LINE

PATTERN OVERLAP LINE

PATTERN OVERLAP LINE

CUT 5 COMPLETE EAR-
RING HOLDER BARS
FROM 1/4" STOCK

42

COLLAPSIBLE BASKETS

STOCK: 3/4" HARDWOOD

DRILL 1/8" PIVOT HOLE
BEFORE SAWING
BASKET FREE. AFTER
ROUTING 1/4" R
COUNTERSINK FOR
#6 X 1 1/4" F.H. SCREWS

DRILL A 1/16" HOLE TO
START BEVEL SPIRAL
CUT. SAW AT 3 1/2° WITH
TABLE TILTING DOWN TO
THE LEFT AND USING A
#9 OLSON BLADE.

ROUNDOVER
1/4" R

1/8" DRILL &
COUNTERSINK.
ATTACH PIVOT FOOT
WITH #6 X 3/4"
F.H. SCREW

43

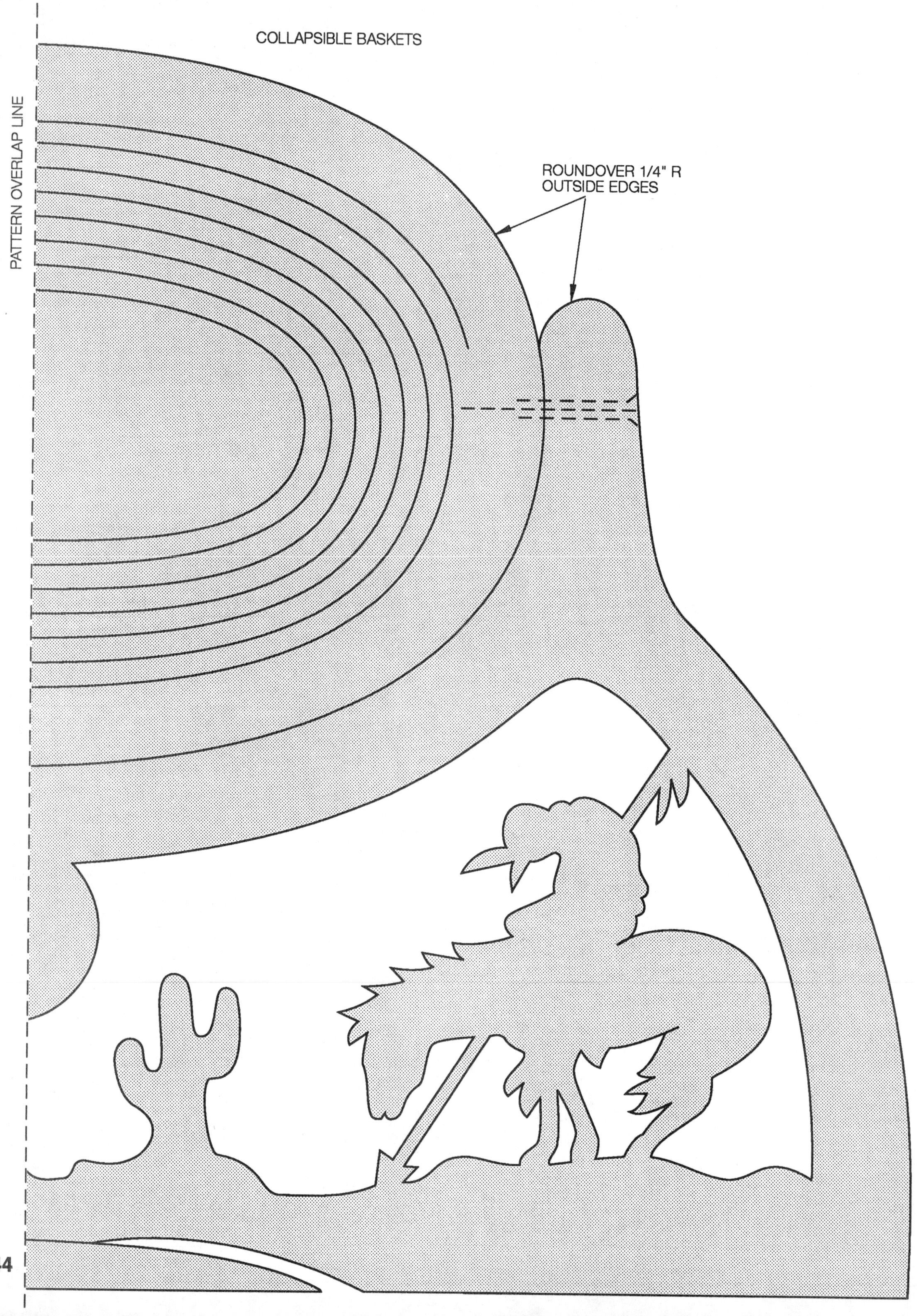

ROUNDOVER 1/4" R
OUTSIDE EDGES

PATTERN OVERLAP LINE

COLLAPSIBLE BASKETS

COLLAPSIBLE BASKETS

STOCK: 3/4" HARDWOOD

DRILL 1/8" PIVOT HOLE
BEFORE SAWING
BASKET FREE. AFTER
ROUTING 1/4" R
COUNTERSINK FOR
#6 X 1 1/4" F.H. SCREWS

DRILL A 1/16" HOLE TO
START BEVEL SPIRAL
CUT. SAW AT 3 1/2° WITH
TABLE TILTING DOWN TO
THE LEFT AND USING A
#9 OLSON BLADE.

ROUNDOVER
1/4" R

1/8" DRILL & COUNTERSINK.
ATTACH PIVOT FOOT WITH
#6 X 3/4" F.H. SCREW

45

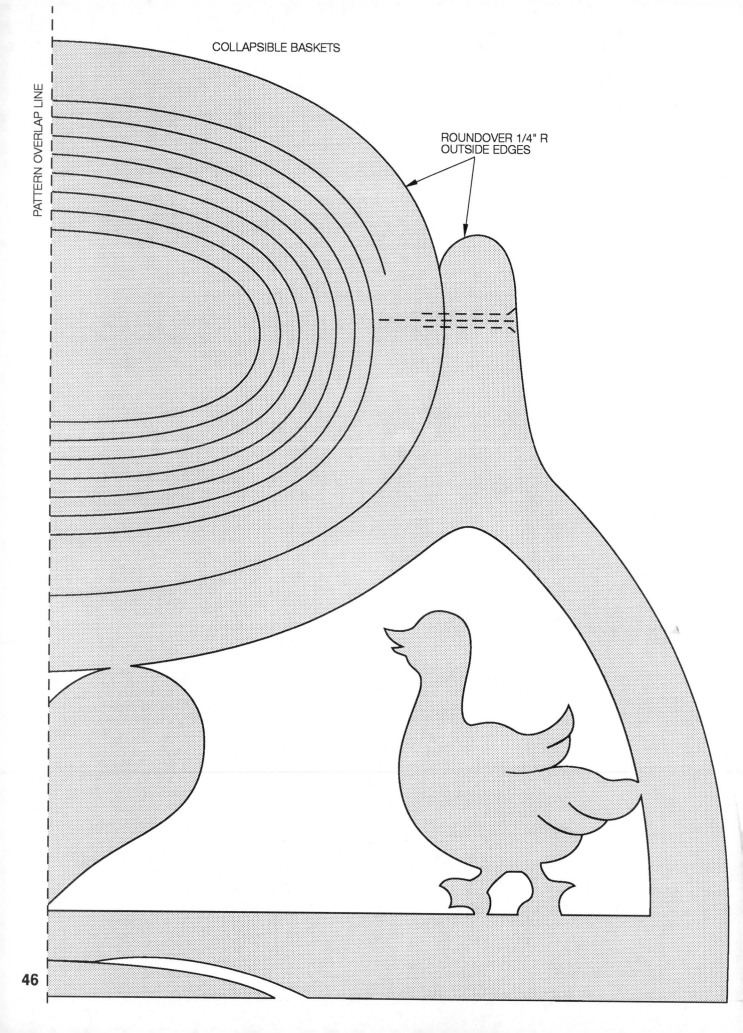

COLLAPSIBLE BASKETS

ROUNDOVER 1/4" R
OUTSIDE EDGES

COLLAPSIBLE BASKETS

COLLAPSIBLE BASKETS

STOCK: 3/4" HARDWOOD

DRILL 1/8" PIVOT HOLE
BEFORE SAWING
BASKET FREE. AFTER
ROUTING 1/4" R
COUNTERSINK FOR
#6 X 1 1/4" F.H. SCREWS

DRILL A 1/16" HOLE TO
START BEVEL SPIRAL
CUT. SAW AT 3 1/2° WITH
TABLE TILTING DOWN TO
THE LEFT AND USING A
#9 OLSON BLADE.

ROUNDOVER
1/4" R

1/8" DRILL & COUNTERSINK.
ATTACH PIVOT FOOT WITH
#6 X 3/4" F.H. SCREW

47

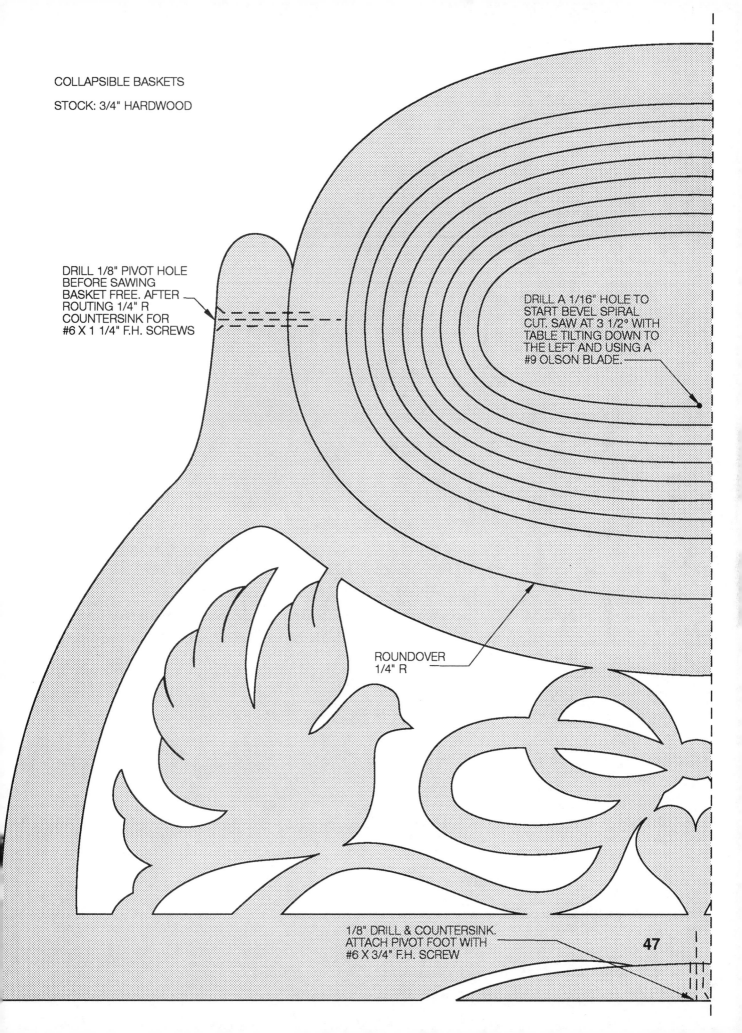

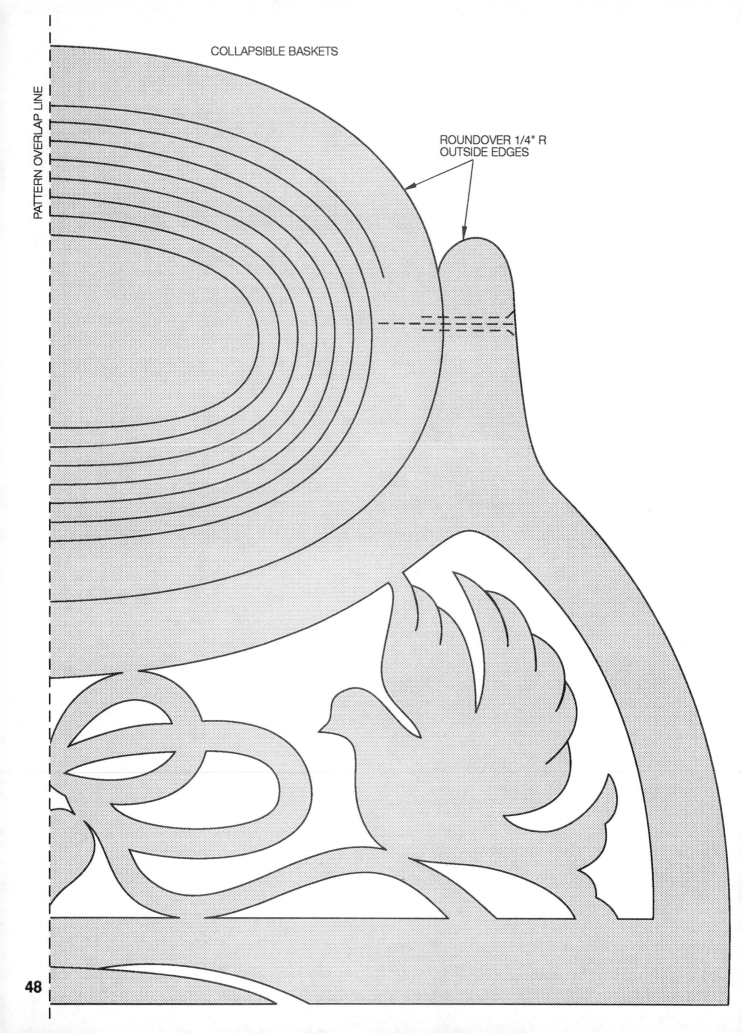

COLLAPSIBLE BASKETS

PATTERN OVERLAP LINE

ROUNDOVER 1/4" R
OUTSIDE EDGES

COLLAPSIBLE BASKETS

48

VICTORIAN BASKET

STOCK: 3/4" HARDWOOD

DRILL 1/8" PIVOT HOLE
BEFORE SAWING
BASKET FREE. AFTER
ROUTING 1/4" R
COUNTERSINK FOR
#6 X 1 1/4" F.H. SCREWS

DRILL A 1/16" HOLE TO
START BEVEL SPIRAL
CUT. SAW AT 3 1/2° WITH
TABLE TILTING DOWN TO
THE LEFT AND USING A
#9 OLSON BLADE.

1/8" DRILL &
COUNTERSINK.
ATTACH PIVOT FOOT
WITH #6 X 3/4" F.H.
SCREW

PATTERN OVERLAP LINE

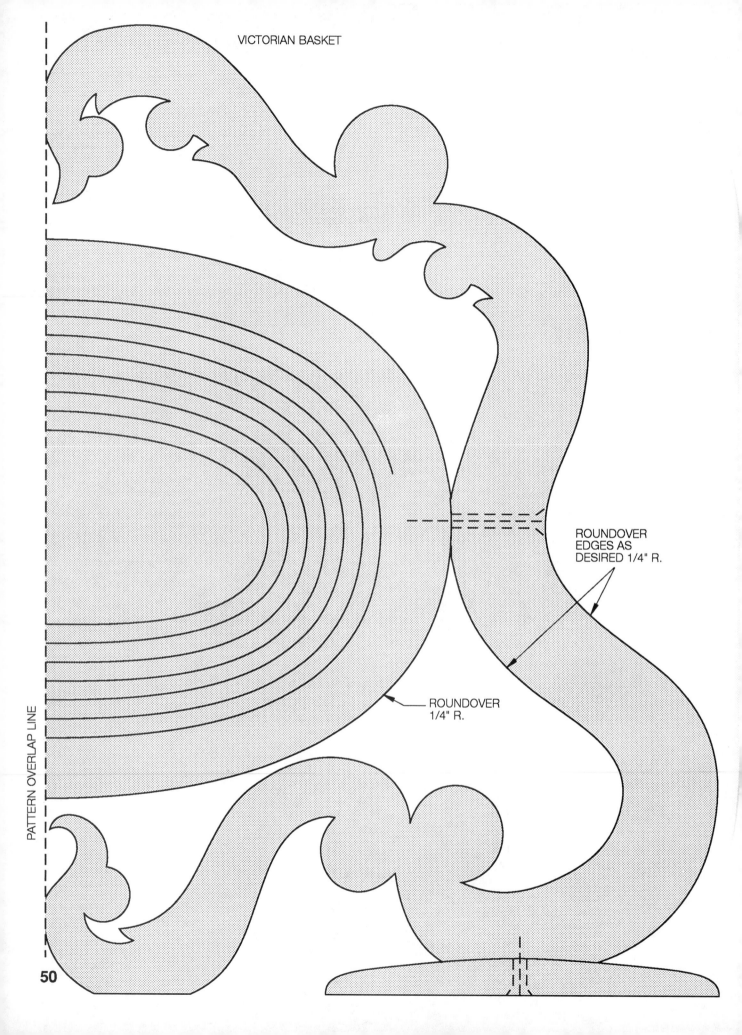

VICTORIAN BASKET

ROUNDOVER
EDGES AS
DESIRED 1/4" R.

ROUNDOVER
1/4" R.

PATTERN OVERLAP LINE

50

PLANTER BASKET

STOCK: 3/4" HARDWOOD

TOP / BASE PATTERN - CUT 1 EACH

DRILL AND COUNTERSINK BOTTOMSIDE
OF BASE TO ATTACH SIDES WITH
#7 X 1 1/2" F.H. SCREWS.

CUT 2 BLANK ENDS - 3/4" T X 5 3/8"W X 5"H

DRILL A 1/16" HOLE TO START
BEVEL CUT. CUT CLOCKWISE WITH
TABLE TILTING DOWN TO THE
RIGHT AT 3° OR CUT
COUNTERCLOCKWISE WITH TABLE
TILTING DOWN TO THE LEFT AT 3°.

PATTERN OVERLAP LINE

PLANTER BASKET

PATTERN OVERLAP LINE

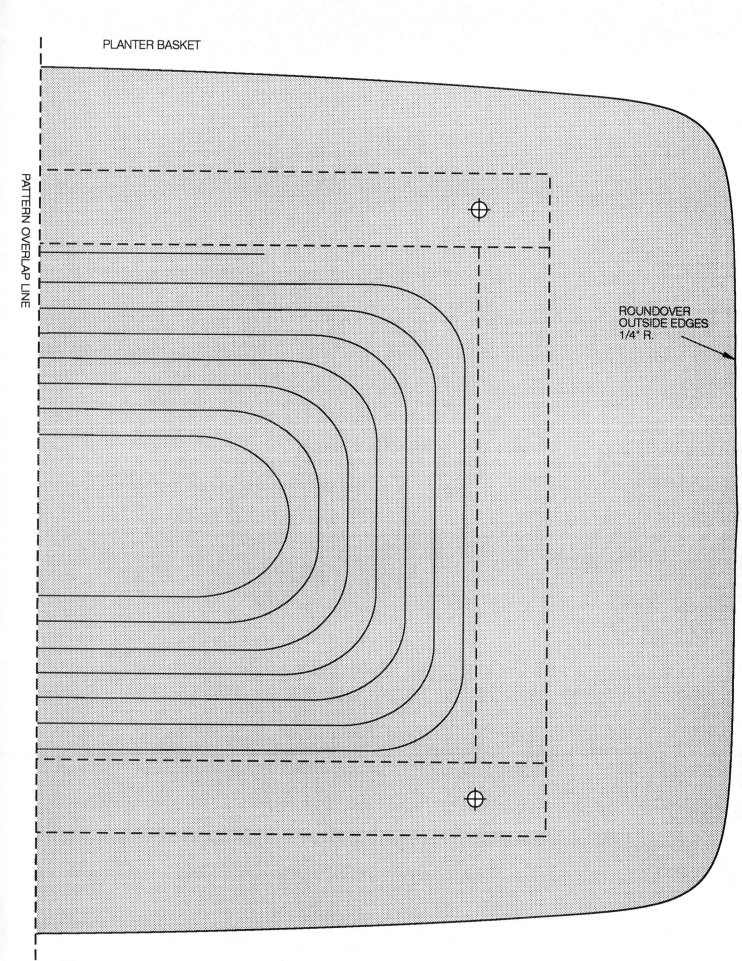

ROUNDOVER
OUTSIDE EDGES
1/4" R.

PLANTER BASKET

INSERT STOCK: 1/4" HARDWOOD
OR PLYWOOD. CUT 2

PLANTER BASKET

INSERT STOCK: 1/4" HARWOOD
OR PLYWOOD. CUT 2

PLANTER BASKET

INSERT STOCK: 1/4" HARDWOOD
OR PLYWOOD. CUT 2

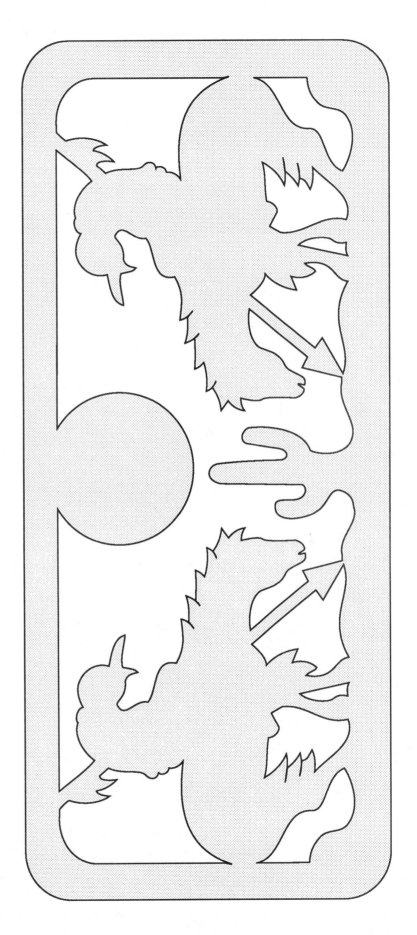

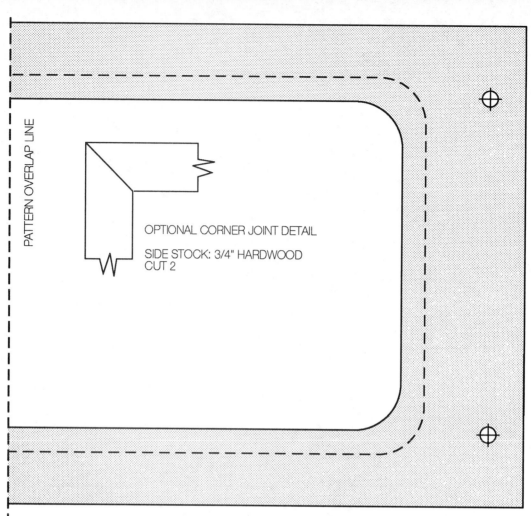

OPTIONAL CORNER JOINT DETAIL

SIDE STOCK: 3/4" HARDWOOD
CUT 2

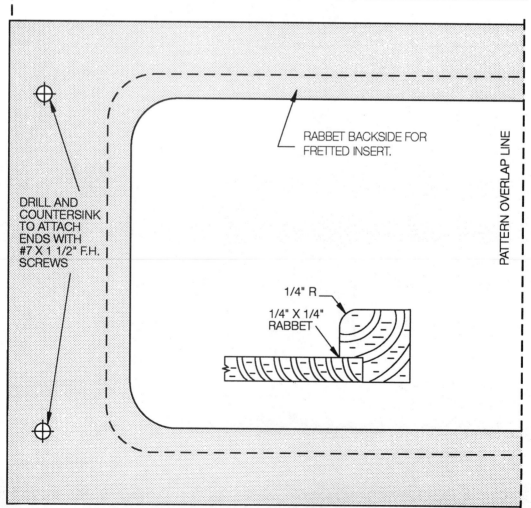

RABBET BACKSIDE FOR
FRETTED INSERT.

DRILL AND
COUNTERSINK
TO ATTACH
ENDS WITH
#7 X 1 1/2" F.H.
SCREWS

1/4" R

1/4" X 1/4"
RABBET

PATTERN OVERLAP LINE

VICTORIAN CLOCK WITH BASKET

STOCK: 3/4" HARDWOOD

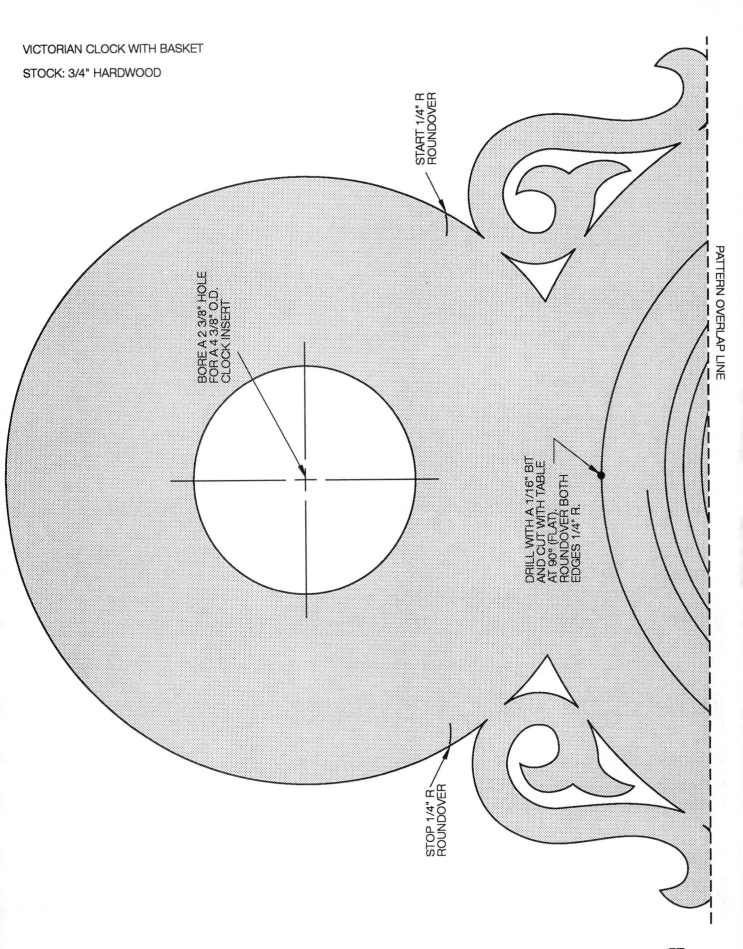

START 1/4" R ROUNDOVER

BORE A 2 3/8" HOLE FOR A 4 3/8" O.D. CLOCK INSERT

DRILL WITH A 1/16" BIT AND CUT WITH TABLE AT 90° (FLAT). ROUNDOVER BOTH EDGES 1/4" R.

STOP 1/4" R ROUNDOVER

PATTERN OVERLAP LINE

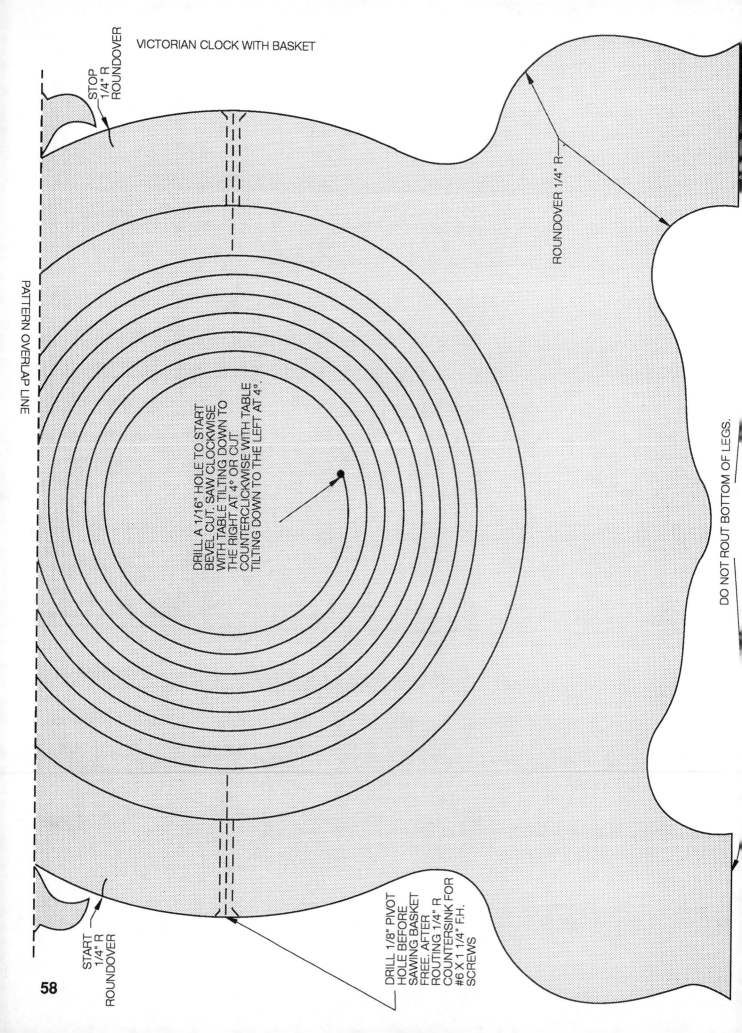

VICTORIAN CLOCK WITH BASKET

STOP
1/4" R
ROUNDOVER

PATTERN OVERLAP LINE

ROUNDOVER 1/4" R

DRILL A 1/16" HOLE TO START
BEVEL CUT. SAW CLOCKWISE
WITH TABLE TILTING DOWN TO
THE RIGHT AT 4° OR CUT
COUNTERCLOCKWISE WITH TABLE
TILTING DOWN TO THE LEFT AT 4°.

DO NOT ROUT BOTTOM OF LEGS.

START
1/4" R
ROUNDOVER

DRILL 1/8" PIVOT
HOLE BEFORE
SAWING BASKET
FREE. AFTER
ROUTING 1/4" R
COUNTERSINK FOR
#6 X 1 1/4" F.H.
SCREWS

58

VICTORIAN CLOCK WITH BASKET

BASE STOCK: 3/4" HARDWOOD

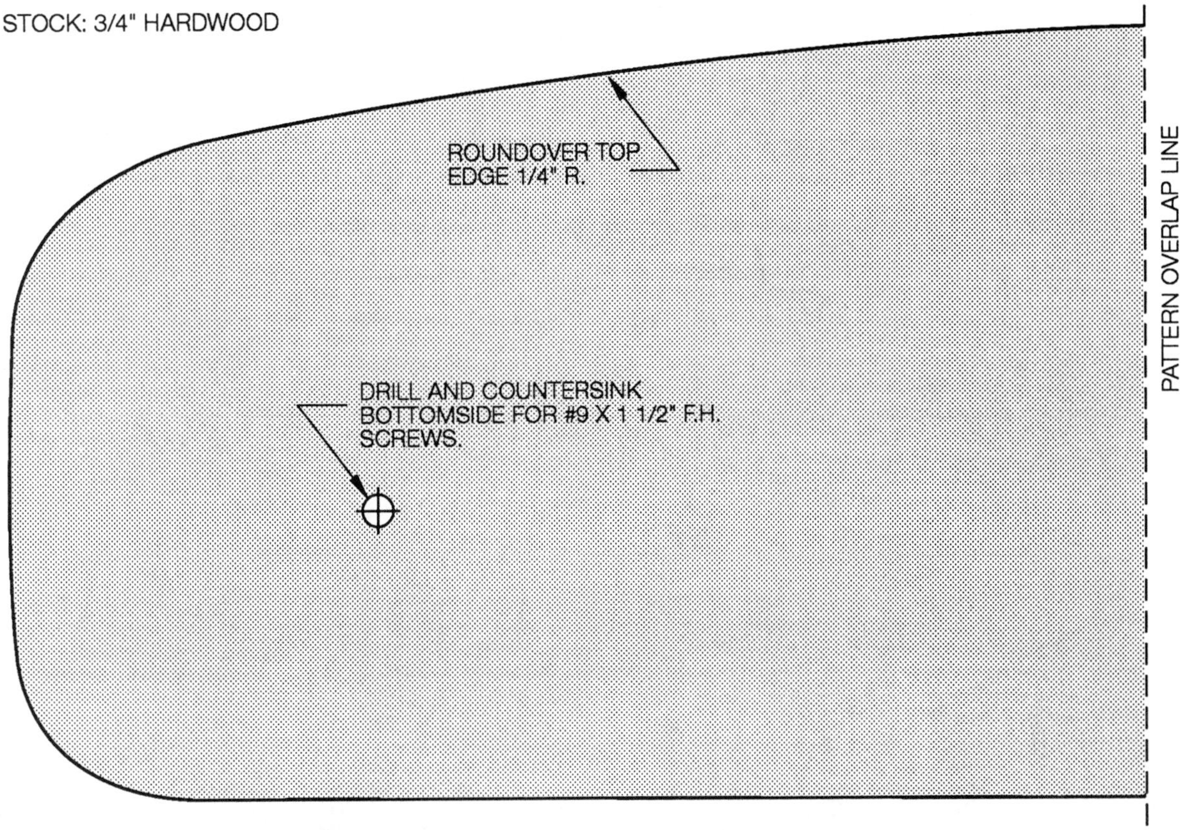

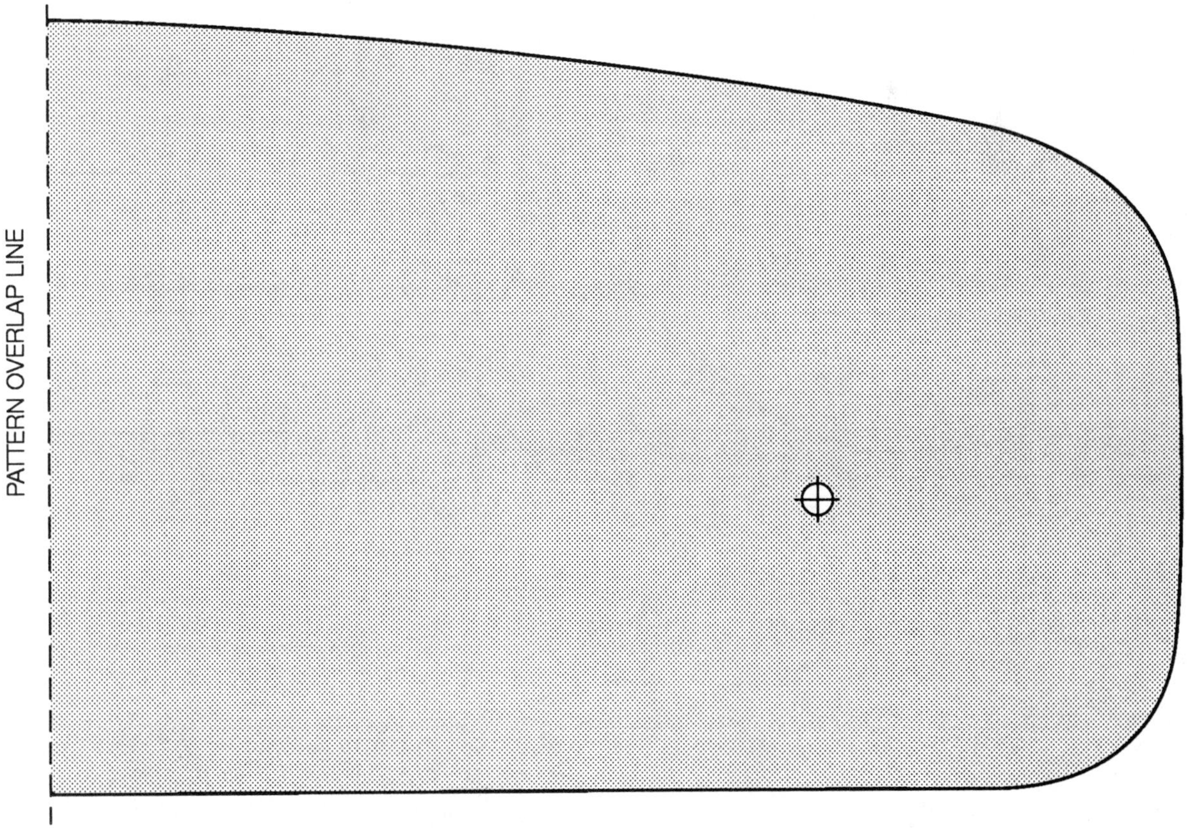

ROUNDOVER TOP EDGE 1/4" R.
DRILL AND COUNTERSINK BOTTOMSIDE FOR #9 X 1 1/2" F.H. SCREWS.
PATTERN OVERLAP LINE

PATTERN OVERLAP LINE

BORE A 2 3/8" HOLE
FOR A 4 3/8" O. D.
CLOCK INSERT

PATTERN OVERLAP LINE

ROUNDOVER FRONT
EDGES 1/4" R.

INSERT STOCK: 1/4" HARDWOOD
OR PLYWOOD

1/4" R   1/4" R

3/4"

1/4"

STOCK: 3/4" HARDWOOD

1/4"

RABBET BACKSIDE
FOR FRETTED INSERT

PATTERN OVERLAP LINE

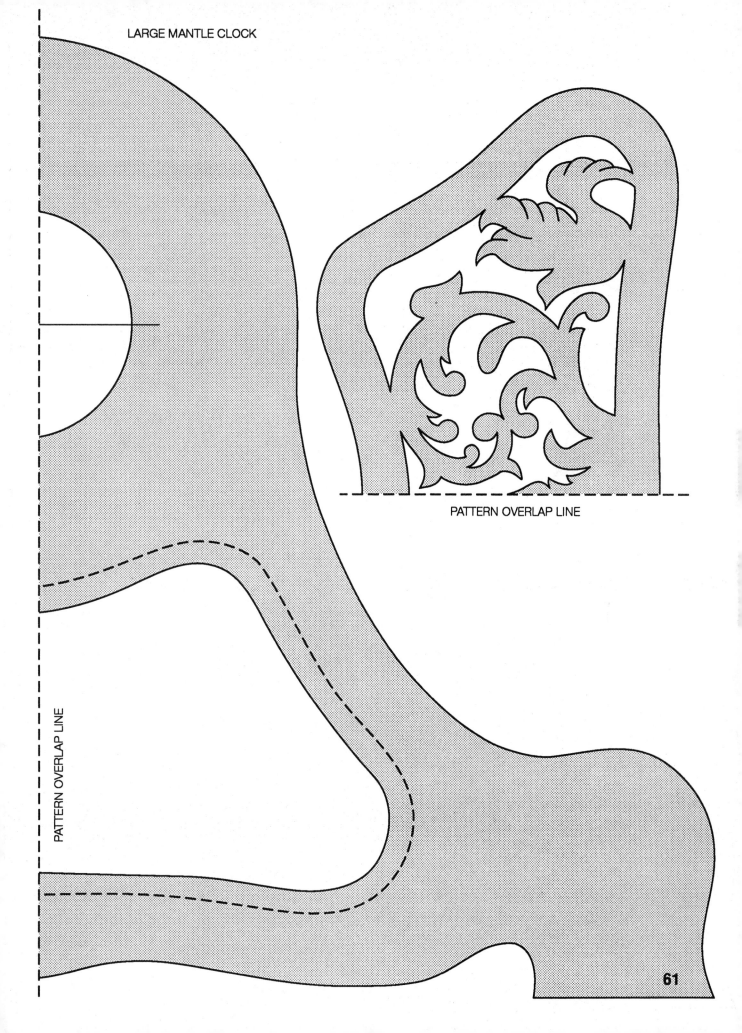

LARGE MANTLE CLOCK

PATTERN OVERLAP LINE

PATTERN OVERLAP LINE

61

LARGE MANTLE CLOCK

INSERT STOCK: 1/4" HARDWOOD
OR PLYWOOD

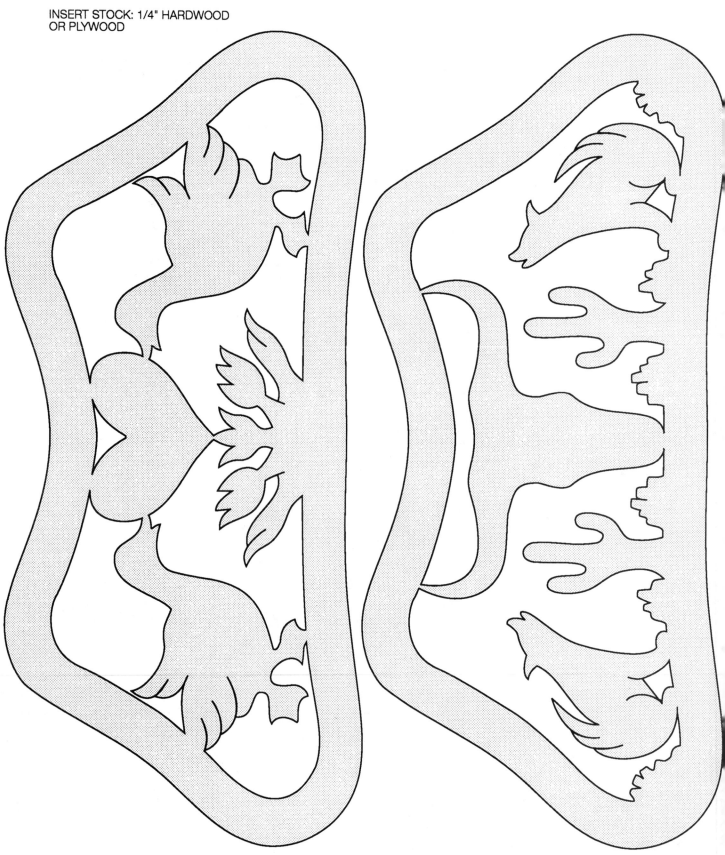

LARGE MANTLE CLOCK

BASE STOCK: 3/4" HARDWOOD

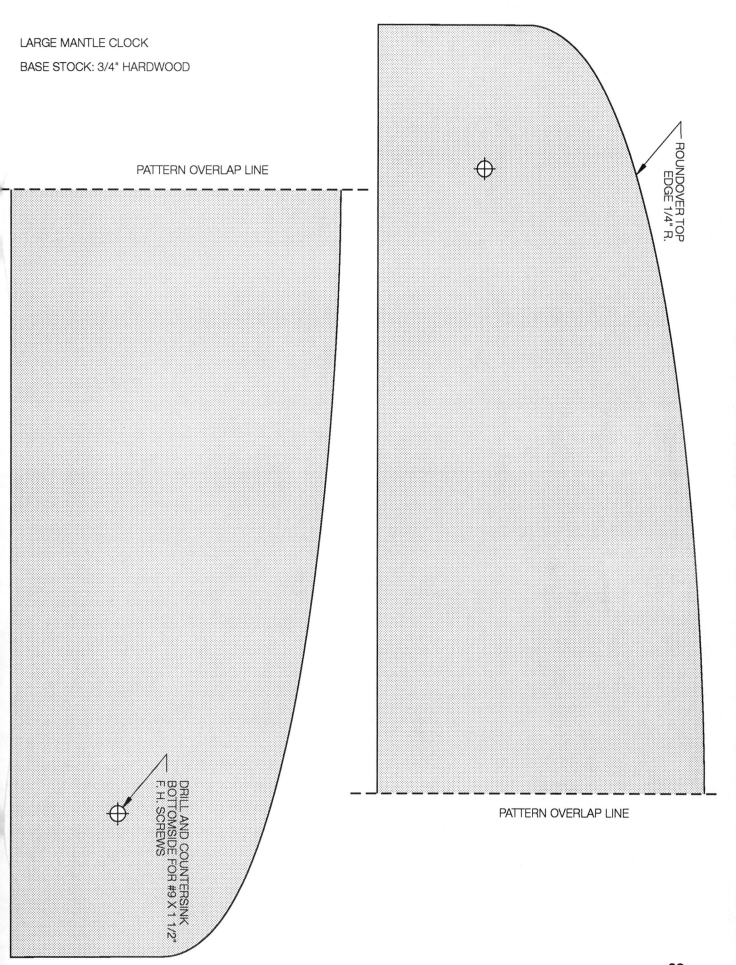

PATTERN OVERLAP LINE

ROUNDOVER TOP EDGE 1/4" R.

DRILL AND COUNTERSINK BOTTOMSIDE FOR #9 X 1 1/2" F. H. SCREWS

PATTERN OVERLAP LINE

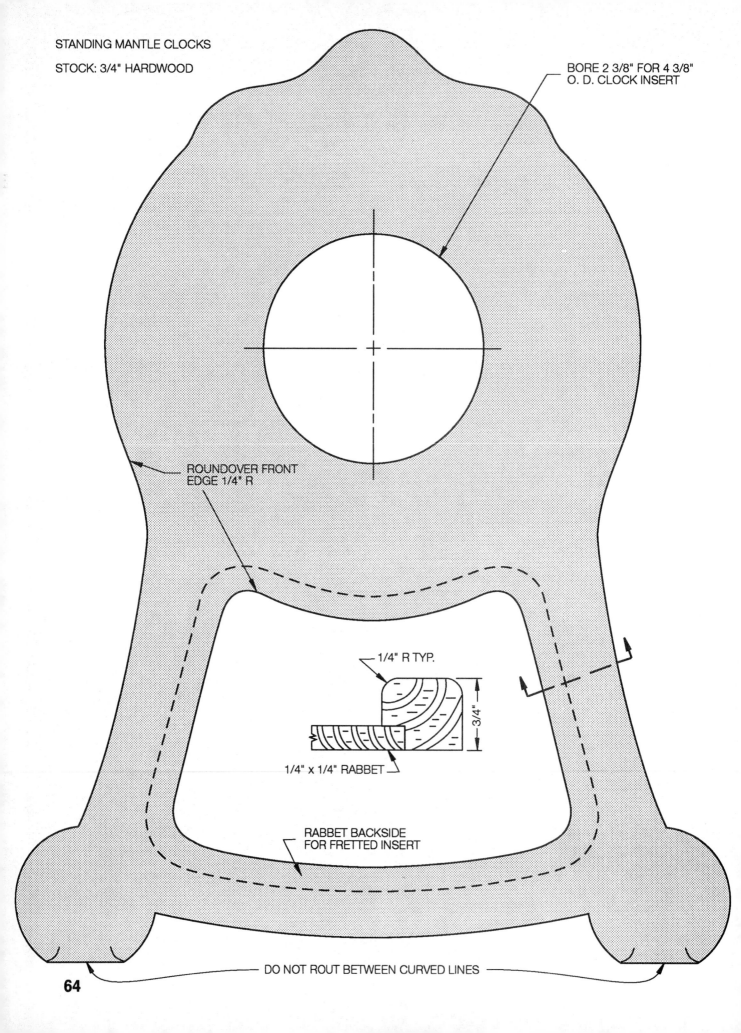

STANDING MANTLE CLOCKS

STOCK: 3/4" HARDWOOD

BORE 2 3/8" FOR 4 3/8"
O. D. CLOCK INSERT

ROUNDOVER FRONT
EDGE 1/4" R

1/4" R TYP.

3/4"

1/4" x 1/4" RABBET

RABBET BACKSIDE
FOR FRETTED INSERT

DO NOT ROUT BETWEEN CURVED LINES

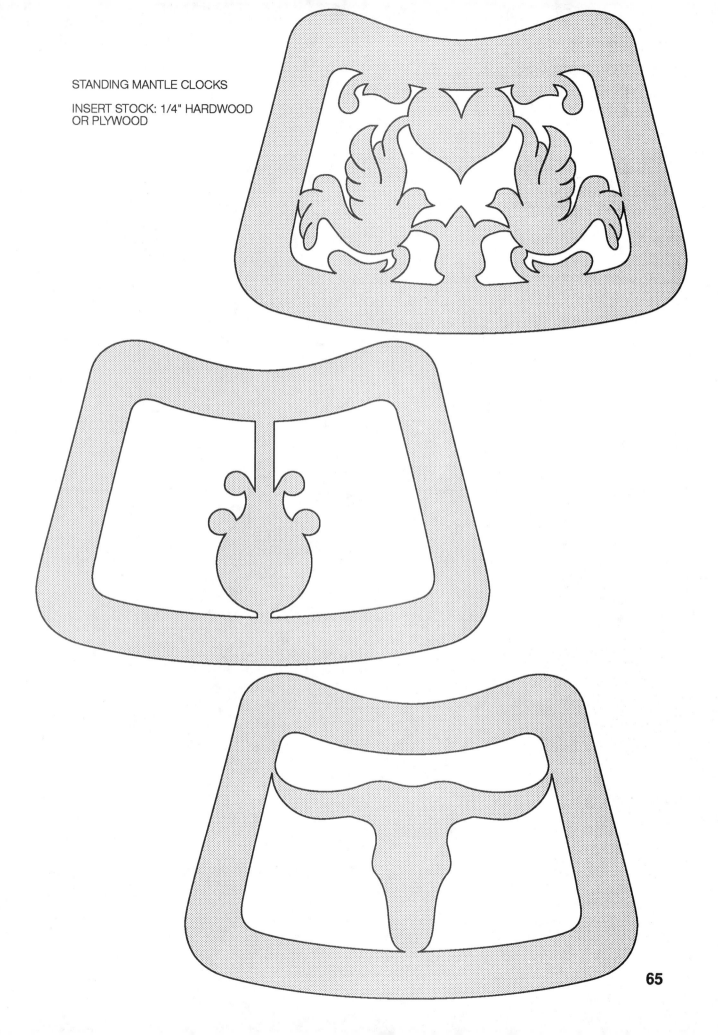

STANDING MANTLE CLOCKS

INSERT STOCK: 1/4" HARDWOOD
OR PLYWOOD

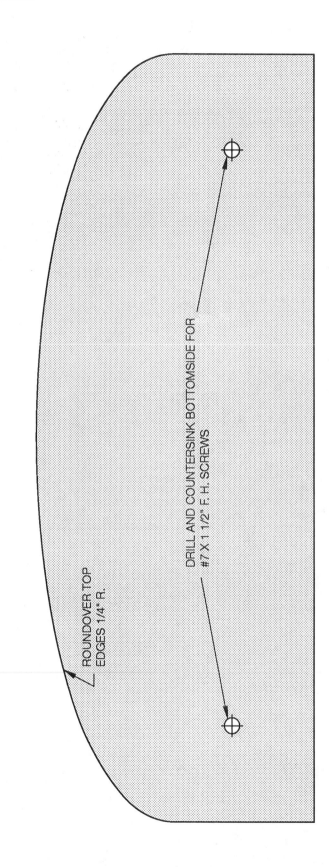

ROUNDOVER TOP
EDGES 1/4" R.

DRILL AND COUNTERSINK BOTTOMSIDE FOR
#7 X 1 1/2" F. H. SCREWS

LARGE DESK SET

STOCK: 1/4" HARDWOOD
OR PLYWOOD

BORE 2 3/8" FOR 2 3/4"
O. D. CLOCK INSERT

LARGE DESK SET

STOCK: 1/4" HARDWOOD
OR PLYWOOD

BORE 2 3/8" FOR 2 3/4"
O. D. CLOCK INSERT

68

LARGE DESK SET

BASE STOCK: 3/4" HARDWOOD

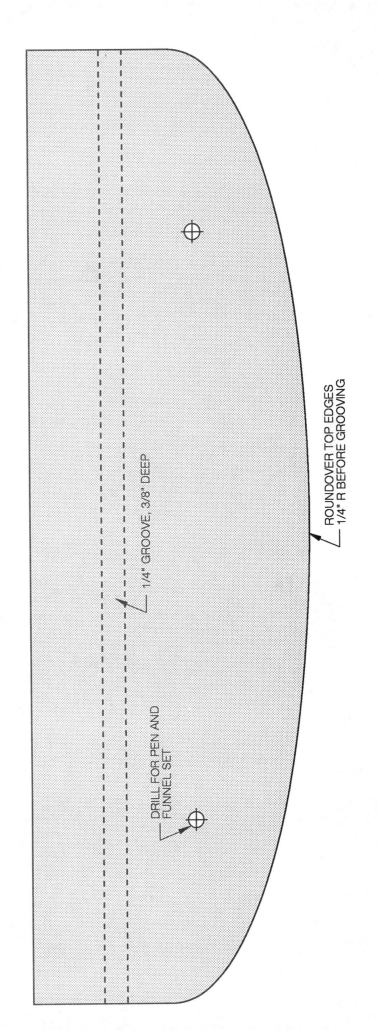

ROUNDOVER TOP EDGES
1/4" R BEFORE GROOVING

1/4" GROOVE, 3/8" DEEP

DRILL FOR PEN AND
FUNNEL SET

VICTORIAN DESK SET

STOCK: 1/4" HARDWOOD
OR PLYWOOD

BORE 1 3/8" HOLE
FOR CLOCK INSERT

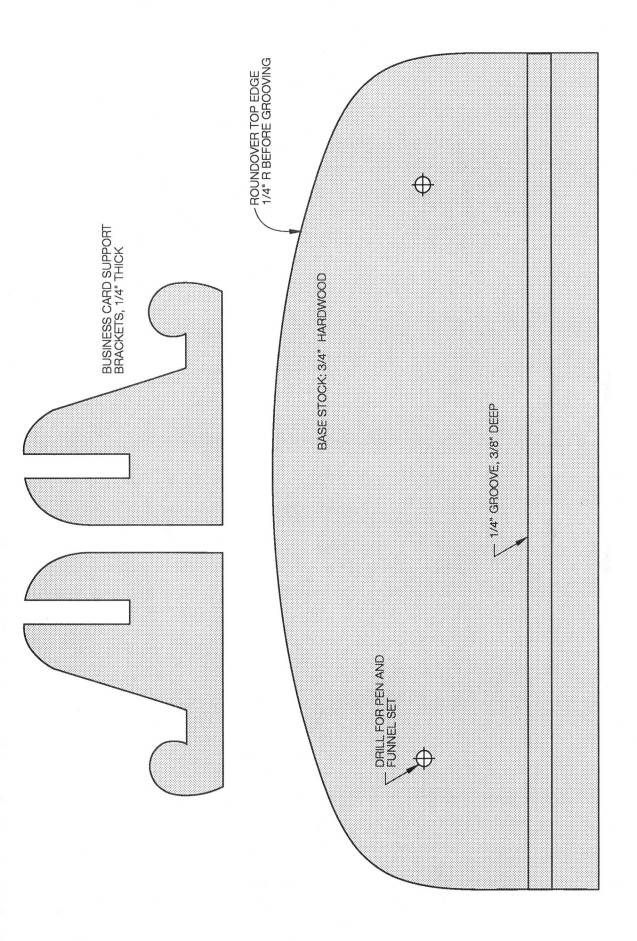

BUSINESS CARD SUPPORT
BRACKETS, 1/4" THICK

ROUNDOVER TOP EDGE
1/4" R BEFORE GROOVING

BASE STOCK: 3/4" HARDWOOD

1/4" GROOVE, 3/8" DEEP

DRILL FOR PEN AND
FUNNEL SET

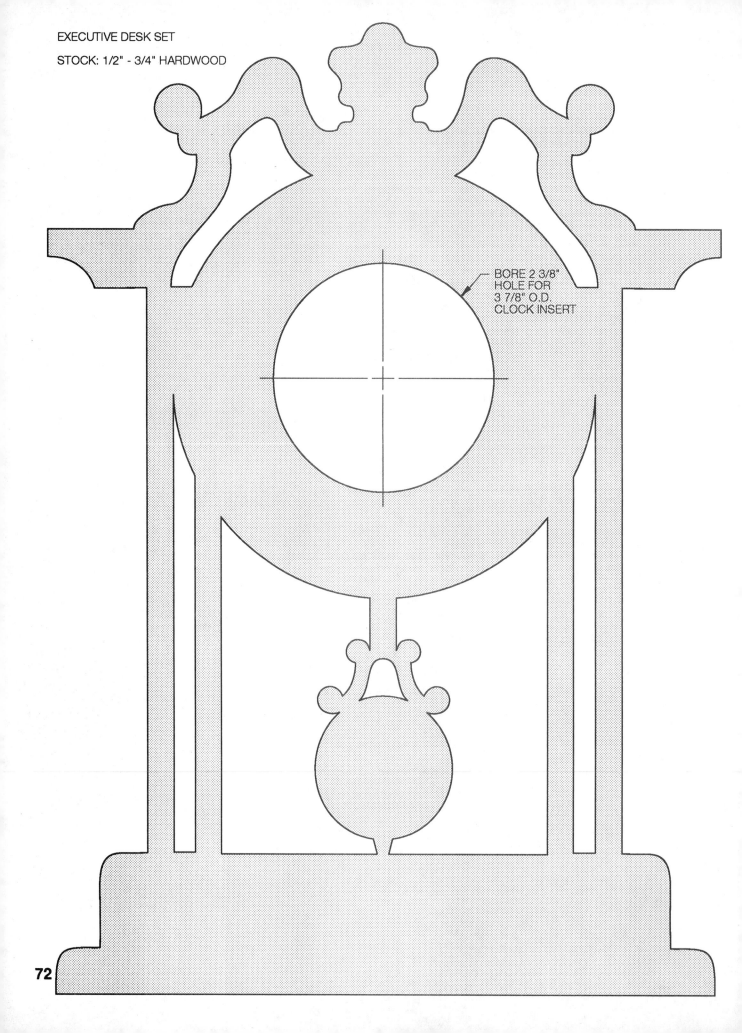

EXECUTIVE DESK SET

STOCK: 1/2" - 3/4" HARDWOOD

BORE 2 3/8"
HOLE FOR
3 7/8" O.D.
CLOCK INSERT

EXECUTIVE DESK SET

BASE STOCK: 1/2" - 3/4" HARDWOOD

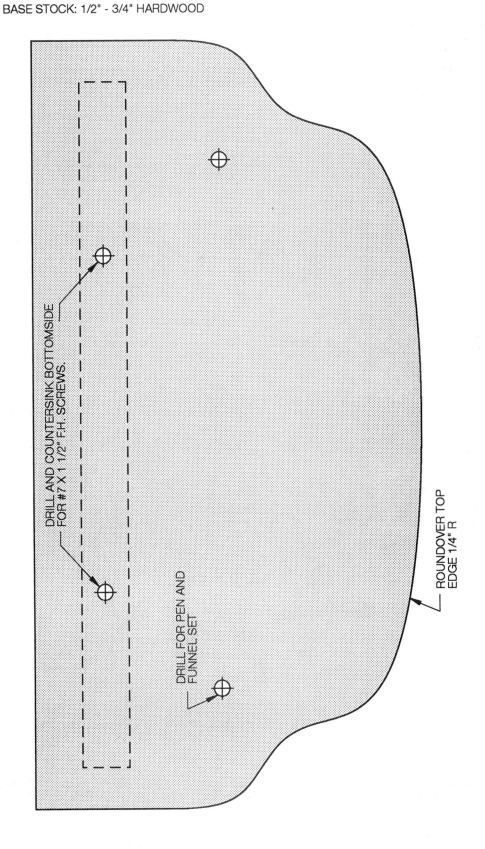

DRILL AND COUNTERSINK BOTTOMSIDE
FOR #7 X 1 1/2" F.H. SCREWS.

DRILL FOR PEN AND
FUNNEL SET

ROUNDOVER TOP
EDGE 1/4" R

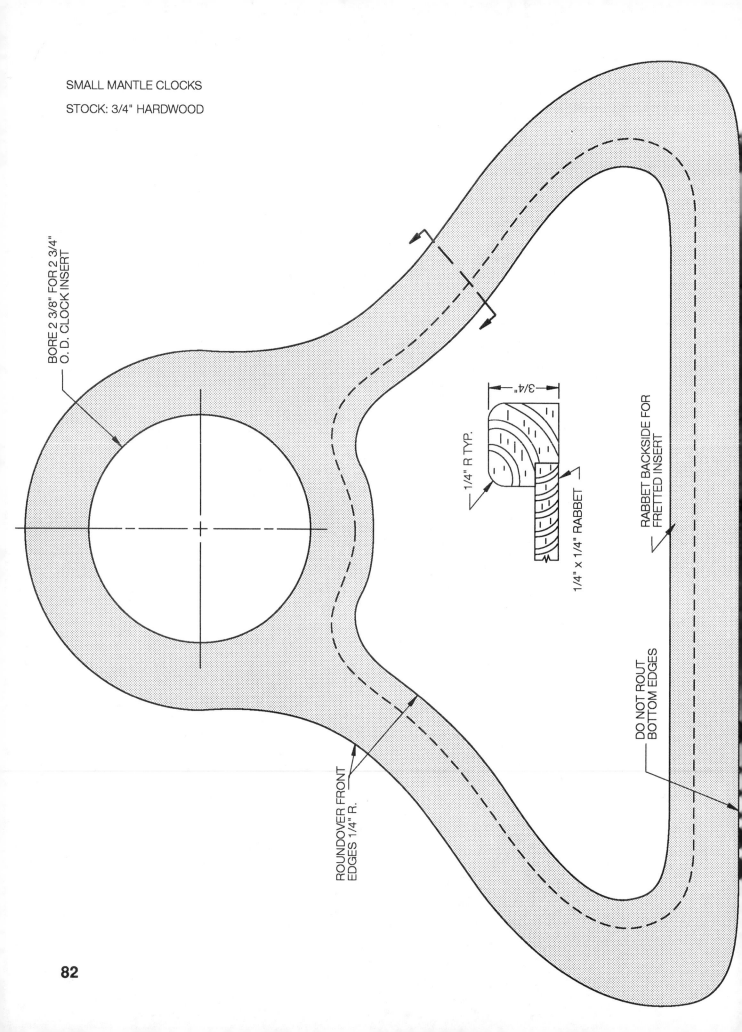

SMALL MANTLE CLOCKS

STOCK: 3/4" HARDWOOD

BORE 2 3/8" FOR 2 3/4" O. D. CLOCK INSERT

ROUNDOVER FRONT EDGES 1/4" R.

1/4" R TYP.

3/4"

1/4" x 1/4" RABBET

RABBET BACKSIDE FOR FRETTED INSERT

DO NOT ROUT BOTTOM EDGES

82

SMALL MANTLE CLOCKS

INSERT STOCK: 1/4" HARDWOOD
OR PLYWOOD

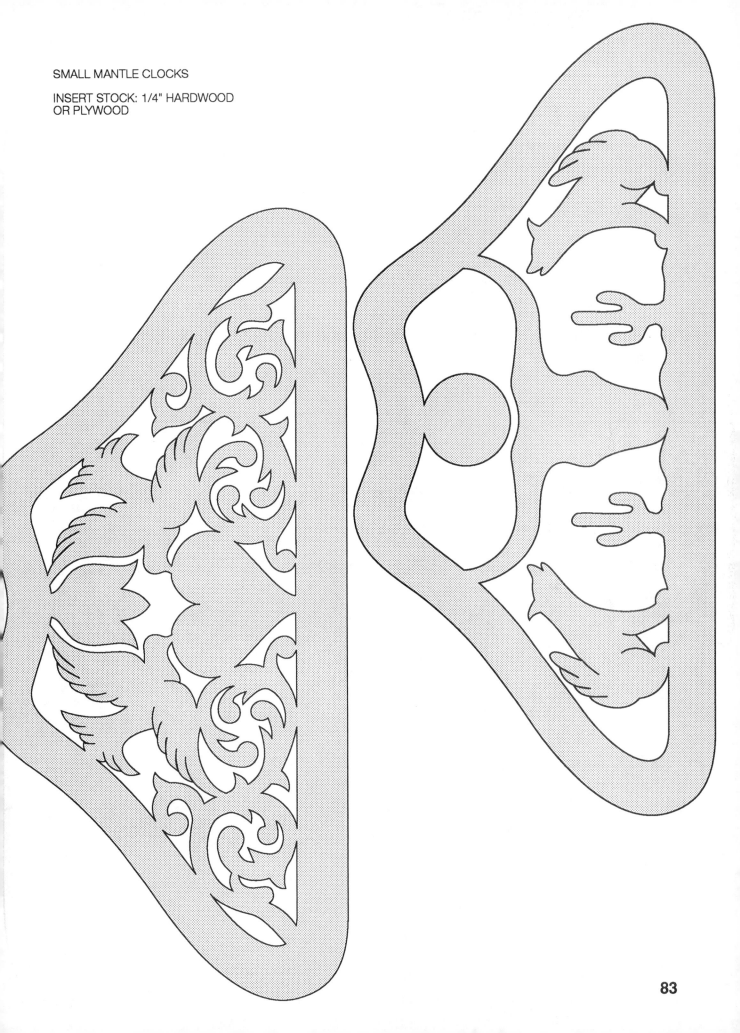

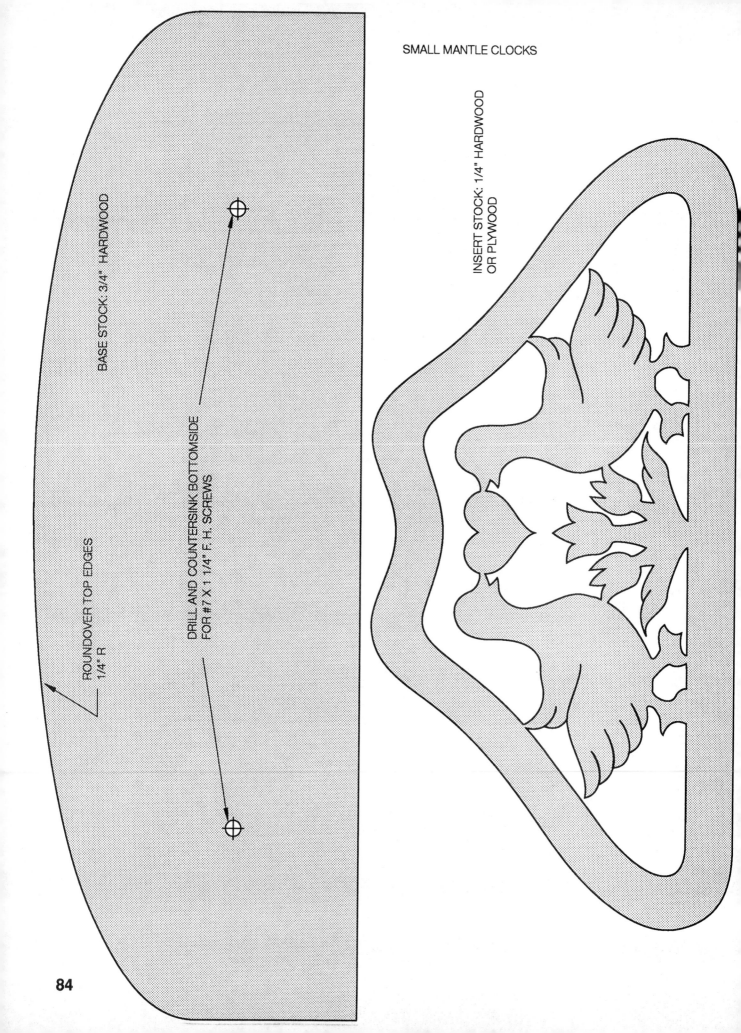

SMALL MANTLE CLOCKS

BASE STOCK: 3/4" HARDWOOD

INSERT STOCK: 1/4" HARDWOOD
OR PLYWOOD

ROUNDOVER TOP EDGES
1/4" R

DRILL AND COUNTERSINK BOTTOMSIDE
FOR #7 X 1 1/4" F. H. SCREWS

84

MINI CLOCKS

STOCK: 1/4" - 3/8" HARDWOOD
OR PLYWOOD

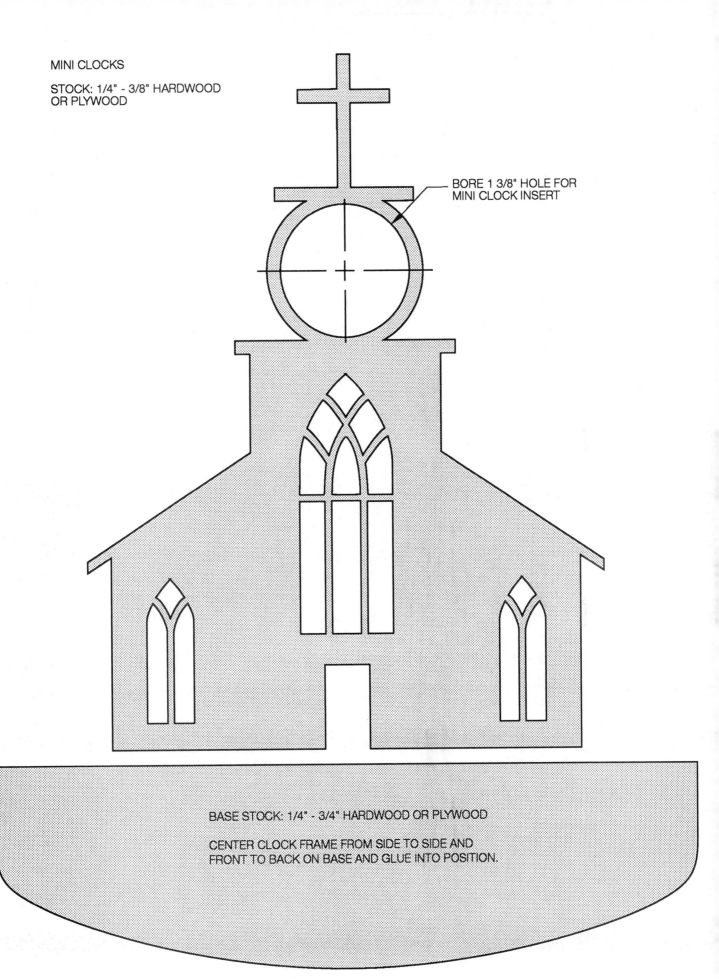

BORE 1 3/8" HOLE FOR
MINI CLOCK INSERT

BASE STOCK: 1/4" - 3/4" HARDWOOD OR PLYWOOD

CENTER CLOCK FRAME FROM SIDE TO SIDE AND
FRONT TO BACK ON BASE AND GLUE INTO POSITION.

MINI CLOCKS

STOCK: 1/4" - 3/8" HARDWOOD
OR PLYWOOD

BORE 1 3/8" HOLE FOR
MINI CLOCK INSERT

BORE 1 3/8" HOLE FOR
MINI CLOCK INSERT

ROCKIN' REINDEER

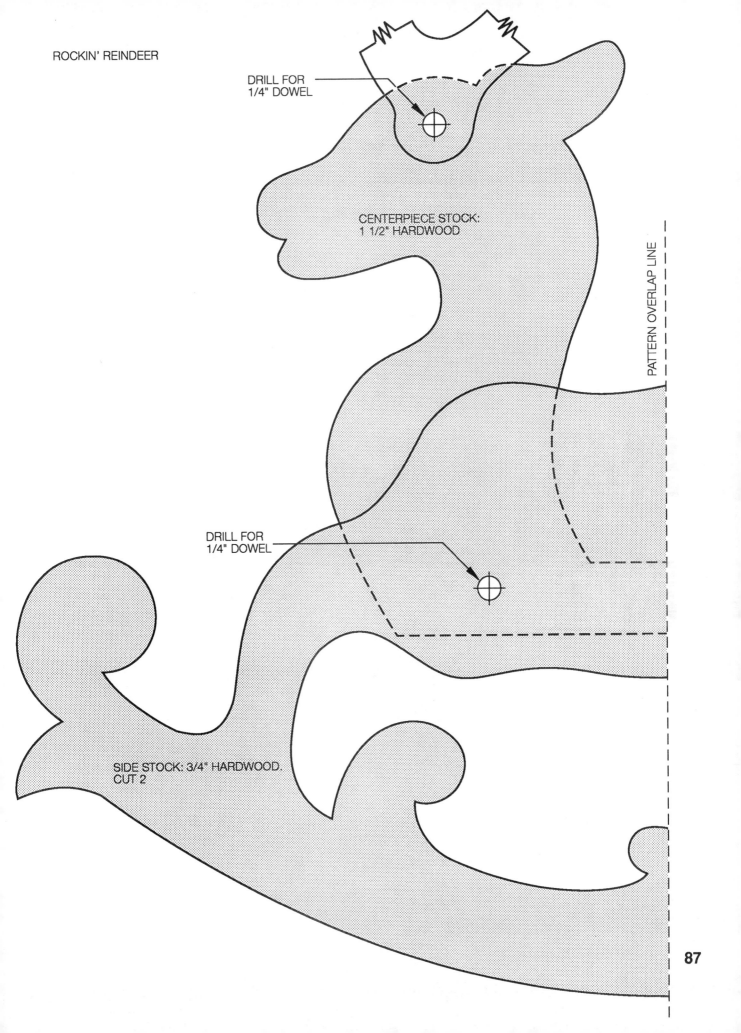

DRILL FOR
1/4" DOWEL

CENTERPIECE STOCK:
1 1/2" HARDWOOD

DRILL FOR
1/4" DOWEL

SIDE STOCK: 3/4" HARDWOOD.
CUT 2

PATTERN OVERLAP LINE

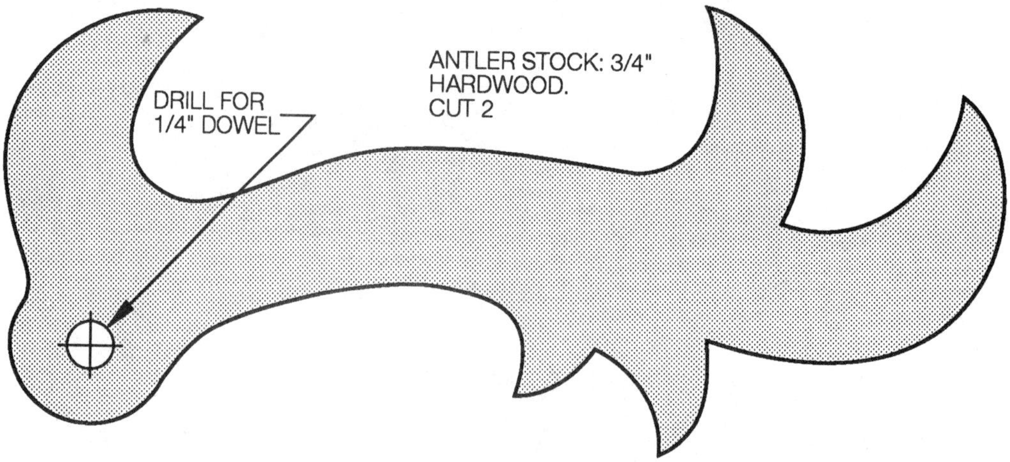

DRILL FOR
1/4" DOWEL

ANTLER STOCK: 3/4"
HARDWOOD.
CUT 2

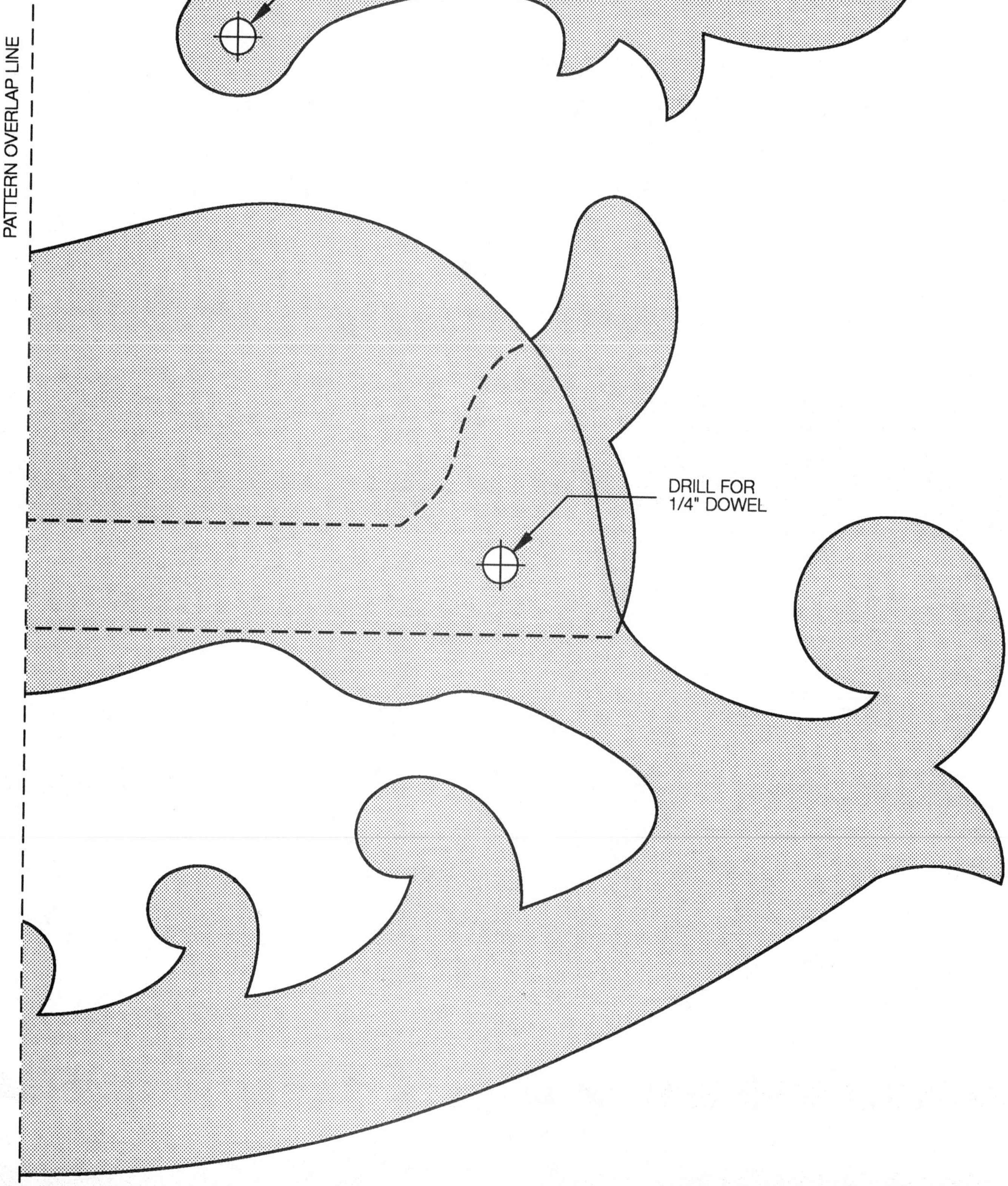

PATTERN OVERLAP LINE

DRILL FOR
1/4" DOWEL

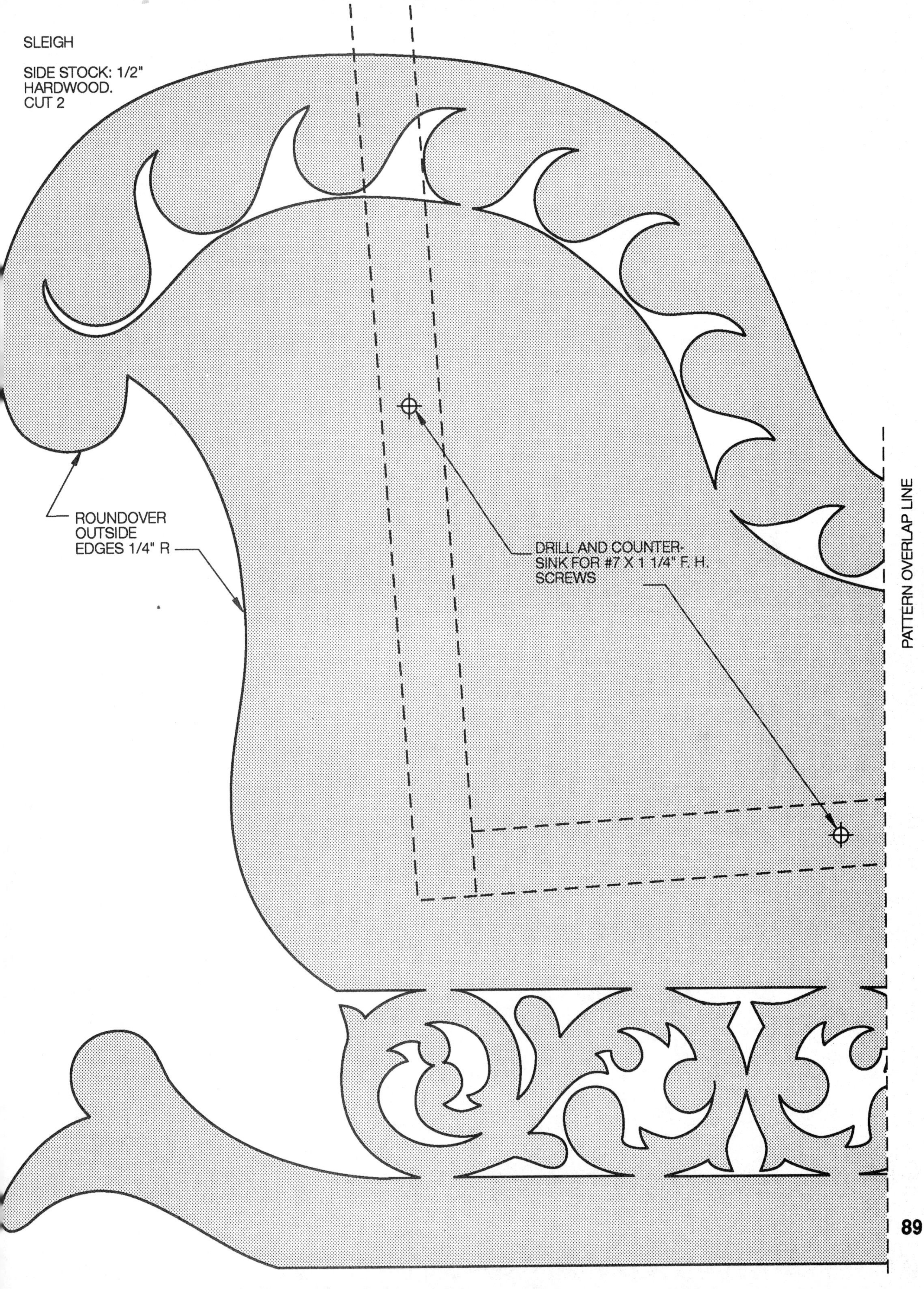

SLEIGH

SIDE STOCK: 1/2"
HARDWOOD.
CUT 2

ROUNDOVER
OUTSIDE
EDGES 1/4" R

DRILL AND COUNTER-
SINK FOR #7 X 1 1/4" F. H.
SCREWS

PATTERN OVERLAP LINE

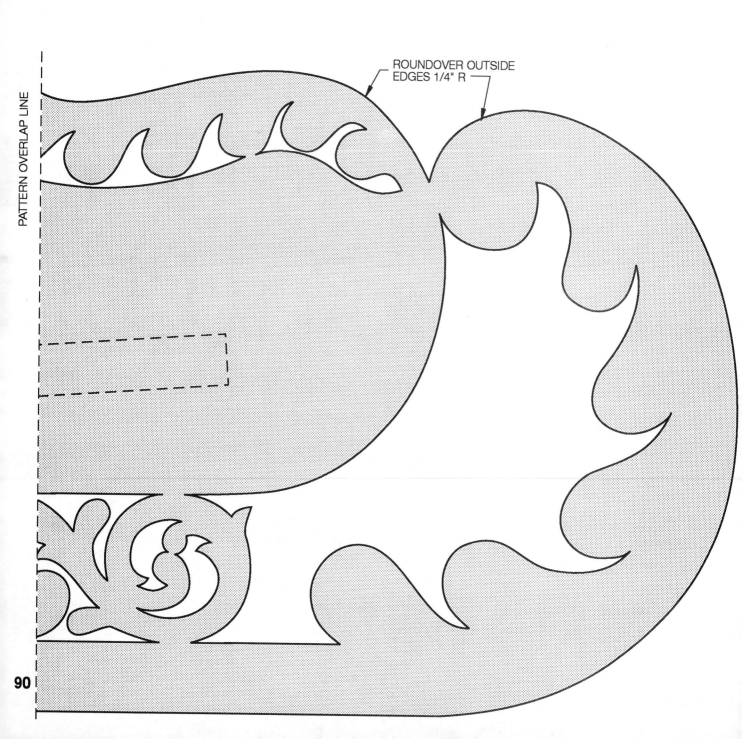

ROUNDOVER OUTSIDE
EDGES 1/4" R

PATTERN OVERLAP LINE

SLEIGH

BACK/SEAT PATTERN - CUT 1 EACH
STOCK: 1/2" HARDWOOD

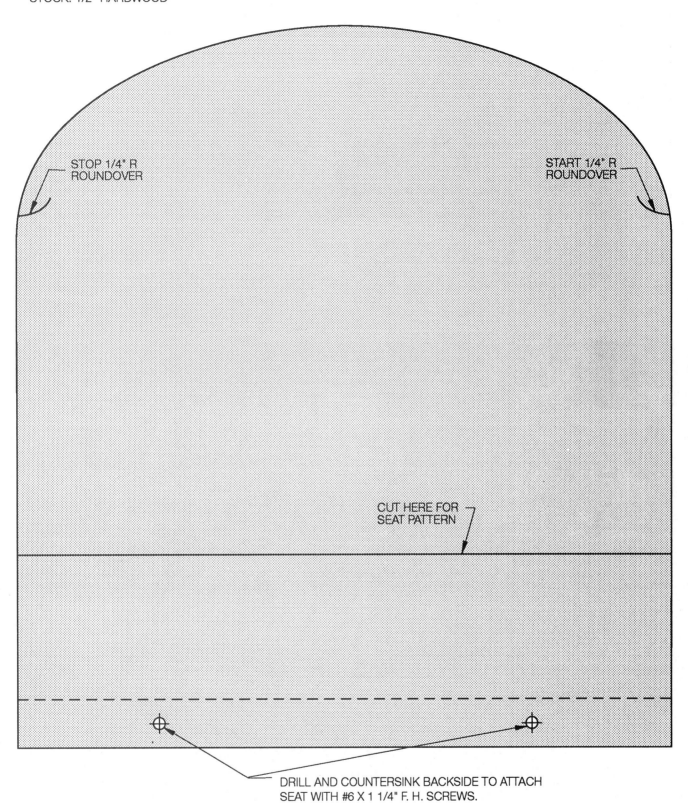

STOP 1/4" R
ROUNDOVER

START 1/4" R
ROUNDOVER

CUT HERE FOR
SEAT PATTERN

DRILL AND COUNTERSINK BACKSIDE TO ATTACH
SEAT WITH #6 X 1 1/4" F. H. SCREWS.

FRAME STOCK: 3/4" HARDWOOD.
CUT 2

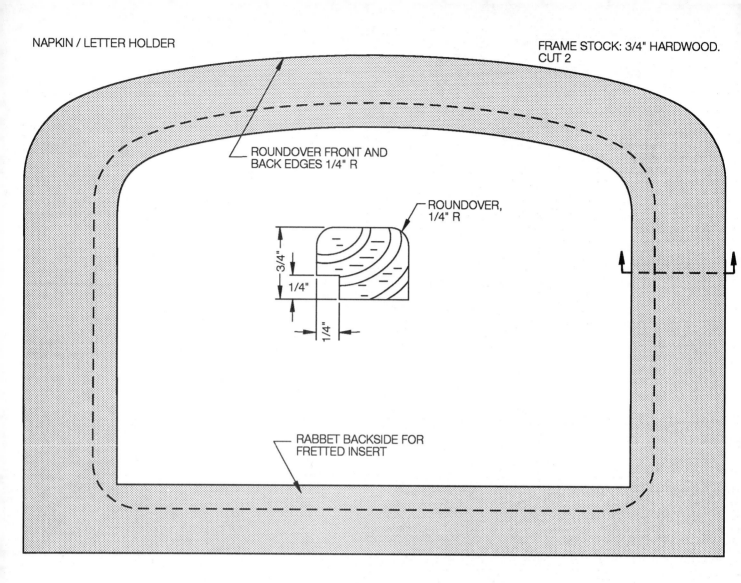

ROUNDOVER FRONT AND
BACK EDGES 1/4" R

ROUNDOVER,
1/4" R

3/4"

1/4"

1/4"

RABBET BACKSIDE FOR
FRETTED INSERT

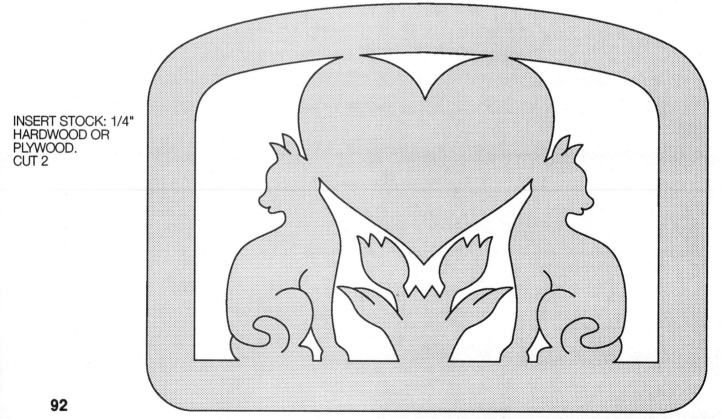

INSERT STOCK: 1/4"
HARDWOOD OR
PLYWOOD.
CUT 2

NAPKIN / LETTER HOLDER

INSERT STOCK: 1/4" HARDWOOD
OR PLYWOOD. CUT 2

NAPKIN / LETTER HOLDER

BASE STOCK: 3/4" HARDWOOD.

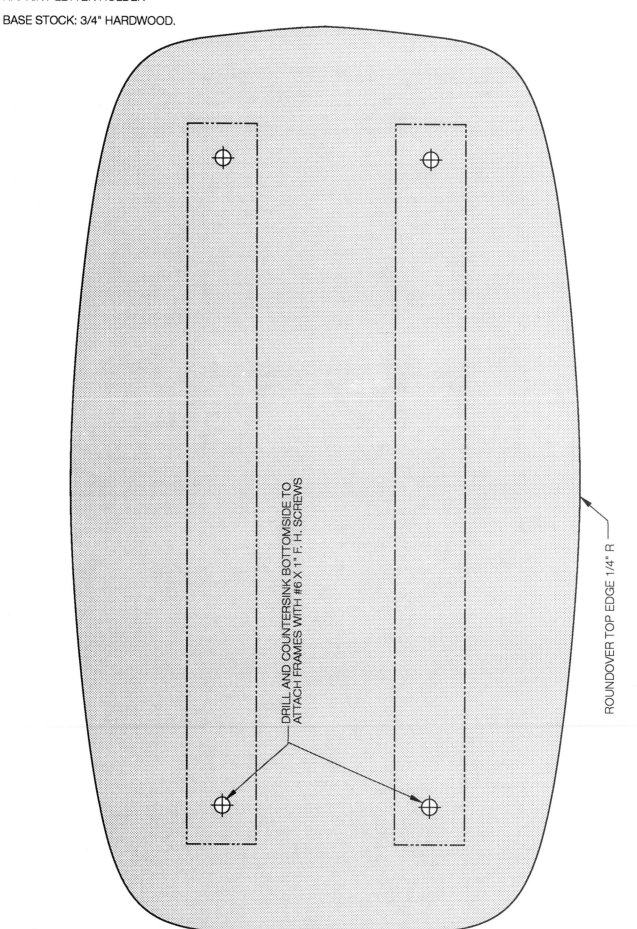

DRILL AND COUNTERSINK BOTTOMSIDE TO
ATTACH FRAMES WITH #6 X 1" F. H. SCREWS

ROUNDOVER TOP EDGE 1/4" R

TISSUE BOX

STOCK: 3/8"
HARDWOOD

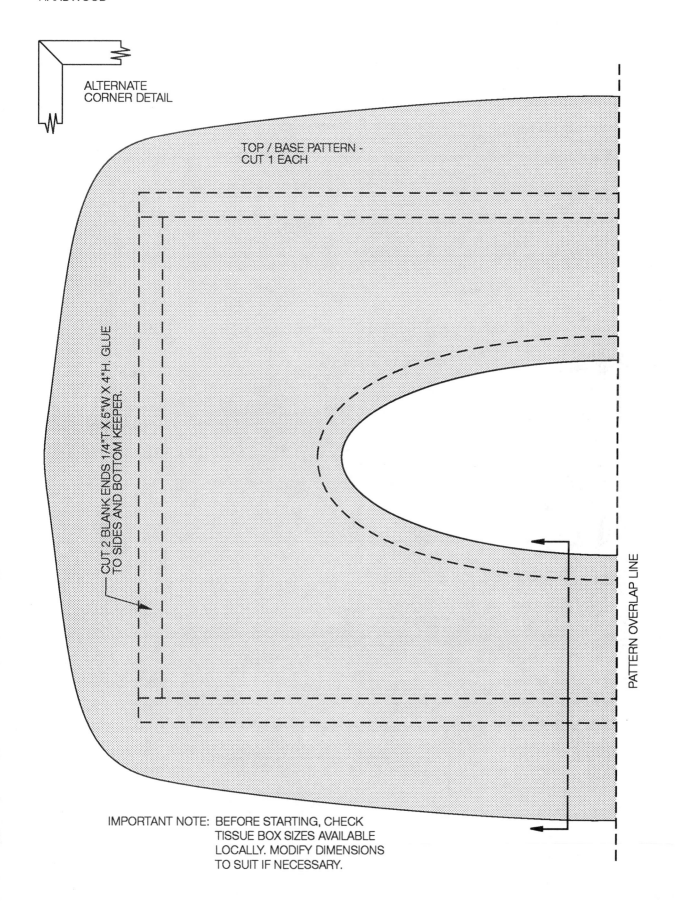

ALTERNATE
CORNER DETAIL

TOP / BASE PATTERN -
CUT 1 EACH

CUT 2 BLANK ENDS 1/4"T X 5"W X 4"H. GLUE
TO SIDES AND BOTTOM KEEPER.

PATTERN OVERLAP LINE

IMPORTANT NOTE: BEFORE STARTING, CHECK
TISSUE BOX SIZES AVAILABLE
LOCALLY. MODIFY DIMENSIONS
TO SUIT IF NECESSARY.

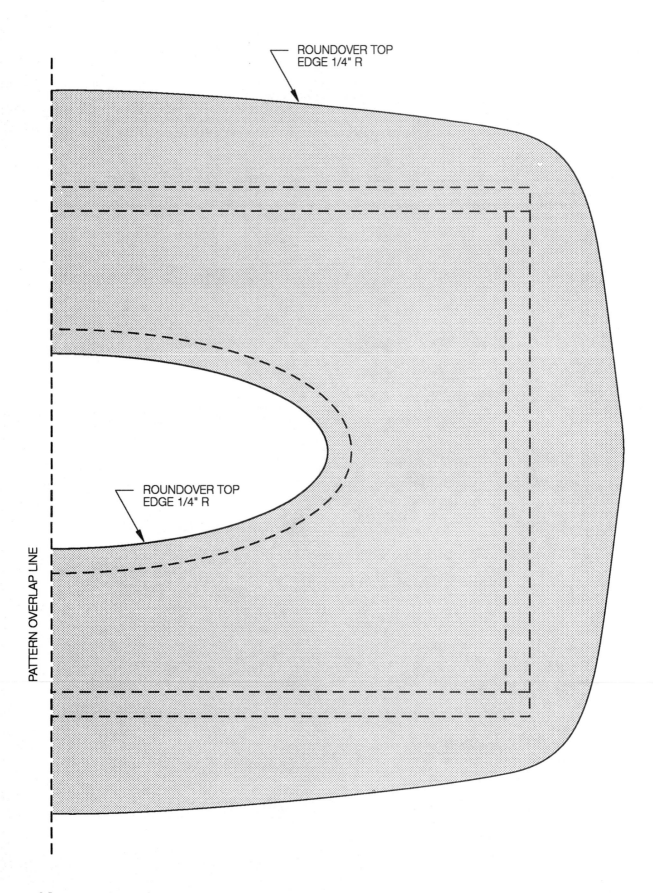

ROUNDOVER TOP
EDGE 1/4" R

ROUNDOVER TOP
EDGE 1/4" R

PATTERN OVERLAP LINE

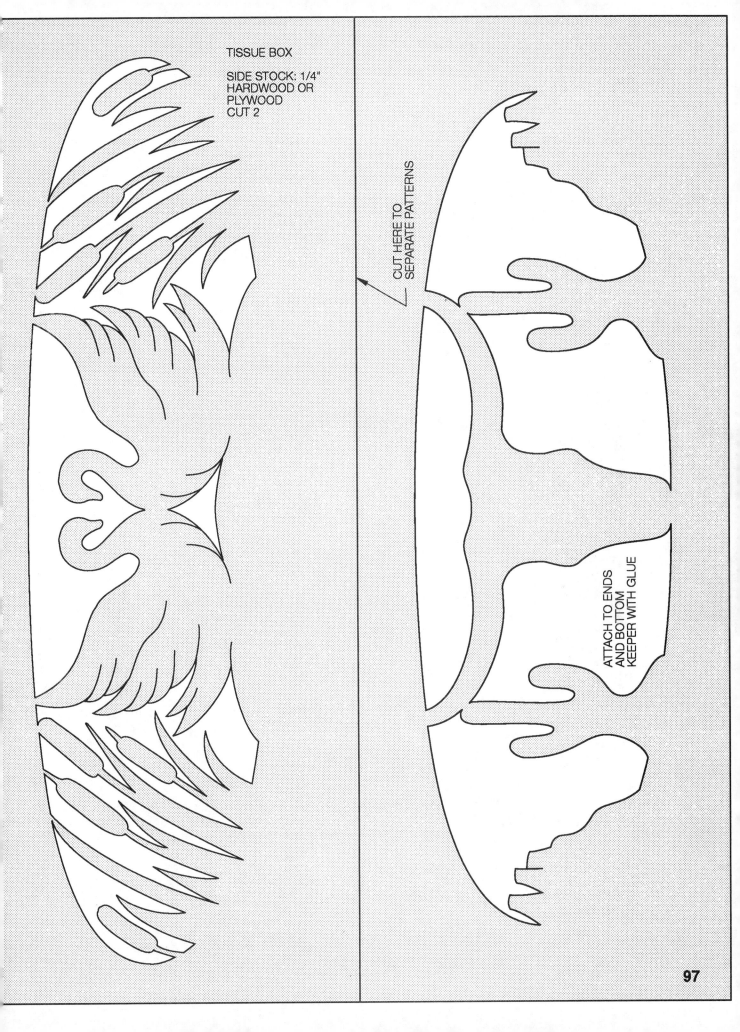

TISSUE BOX

SIDE STOCK: 1/4"
HARDWOOD OR
PLYWOOD
CUT 2

CUT HERE TO
SEPARATE PATTERNS

ATTACH TO ENDS
AND BOTTOM
KEEPER WITH GLUE

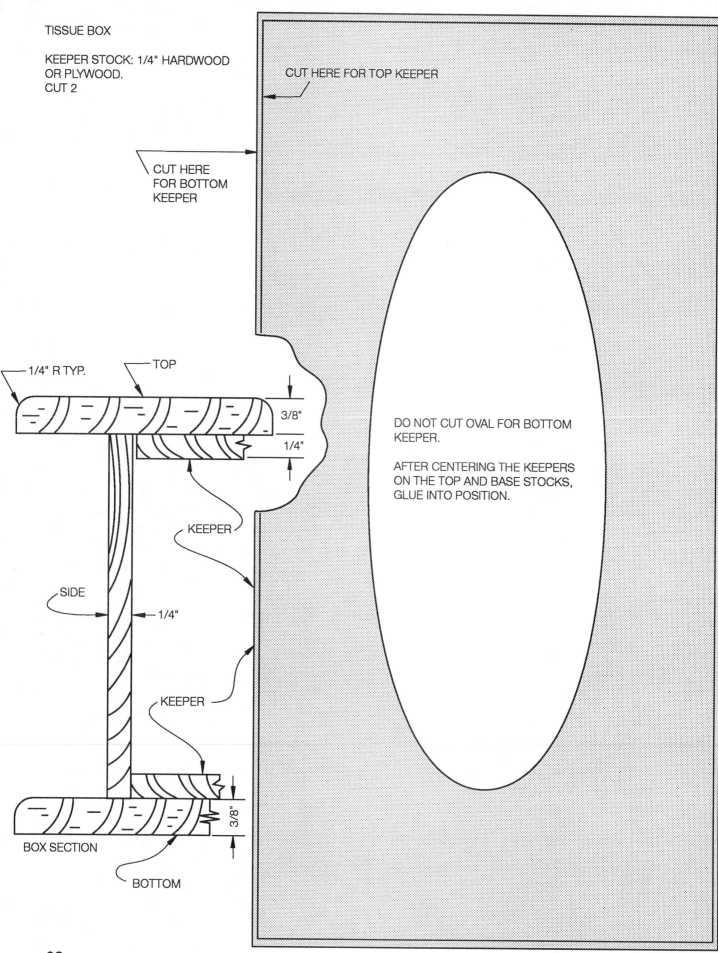

TISSUE BOX

KEEPER STOCK: 1/4" HARDWOOD
OR PLYWOOD.
CUT 2

CUT HERE FOR TOP KEEPER

CUT HERE
FOR BOTTOM
KEEPER

1/4" R TYP.

TOP

3/8"

1/4"

DO NOT CUT OVAL FOR BOTTOM
KEEPER.

AFTER CENTERING THE KEEPERS
ON THE TOP AND BASE STOCKS,
GLUE INTO POSITION.

KEEPER

SIDE

1/4"

KEEPER

BOX SECTION

3/8"

BOTTOM

98

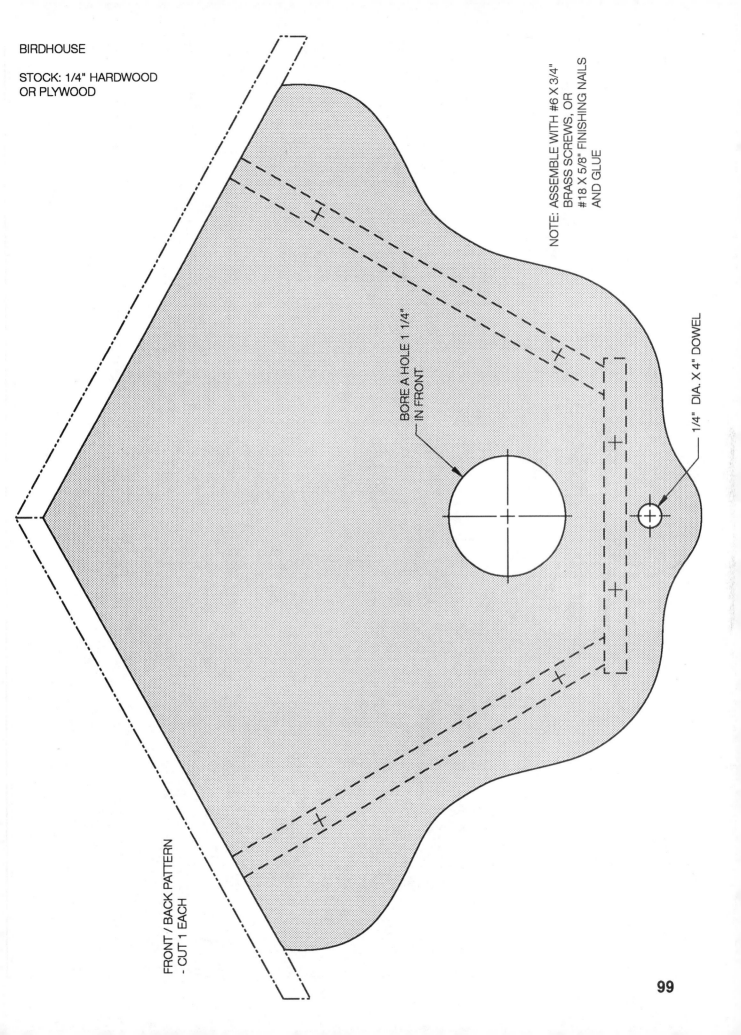

BIRDHOUSE

STOCK: 1/4" HARDWOOD
OR PLYWOOD

NOTE: ASSEMBLE WITH #6 X 3/4"
BRASS SCREWS, OR
#18 X 5/8" FINISHING NAILS
AND GLUE

BORE A HOLE 1 1/4"
IN FRONT

1/4" DIA. X 4" DOWEL

FRONT / BACK PATTERN
- CUT 1 EACH

99

BIRDHOUSE

STOCK: 1/4" HARDWOOD OR PLYWOOD.
CUT 2

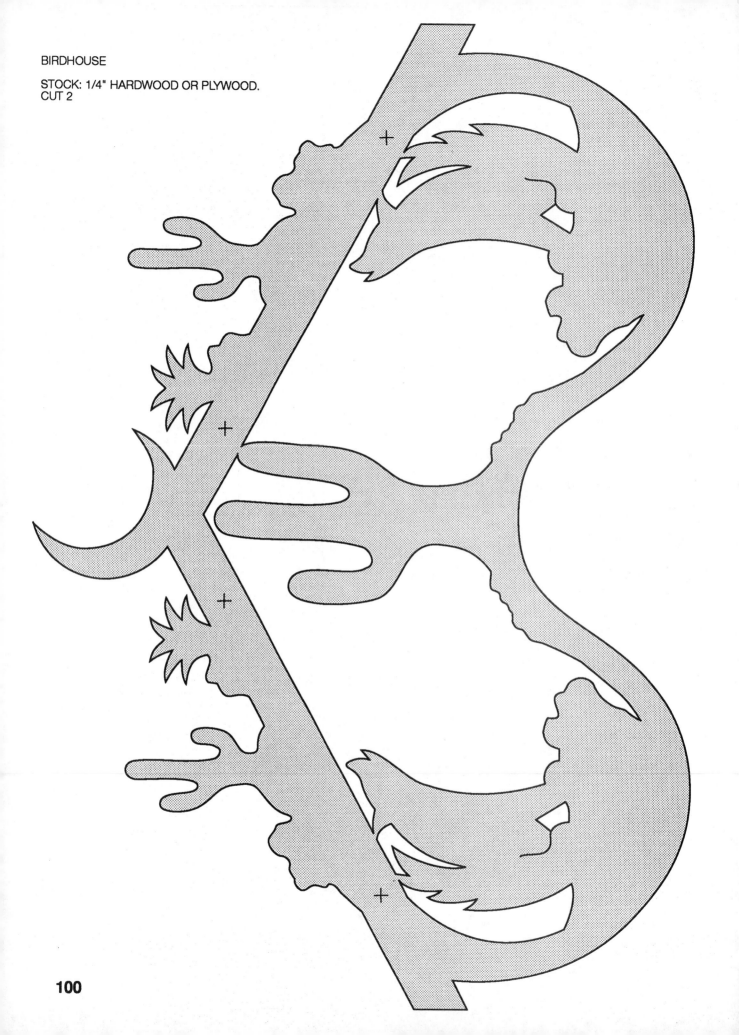

BIRDHOUSE

STOCK: 1/4" HARDWOOD OR PLYWOOD.
CUT 2

BIRDHOUSE

STOCK: 1/4" HARDWOOD OR PLYWOOD

SIDES, CUT 2

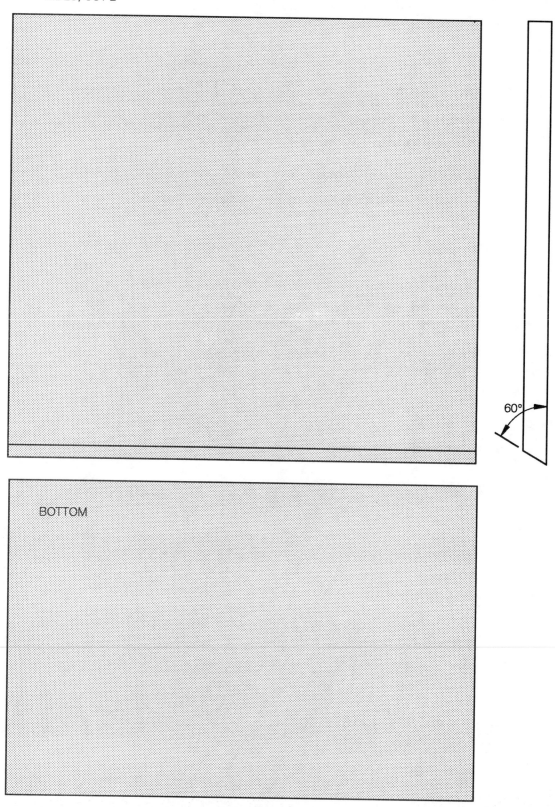

BOTTOM

60°

BIRDHOUSE

STOCK: 1/4" HARDWOOD OR PLYWOOD

ROOF, CUT 2

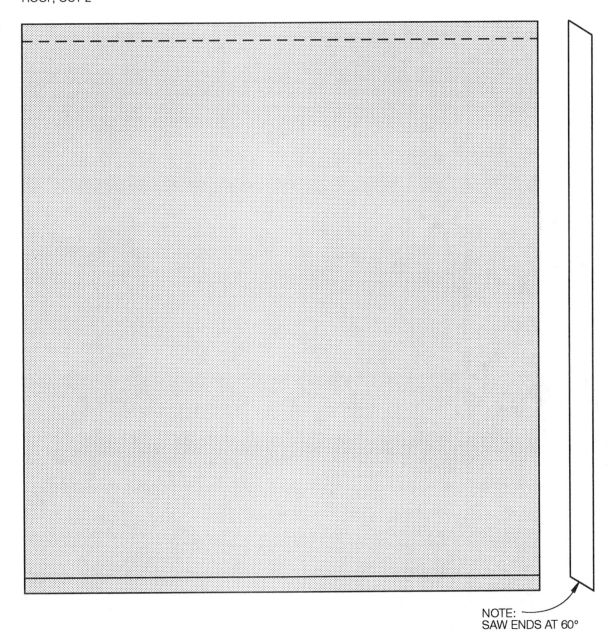

NOTE:
SAW ENDS AT 60°

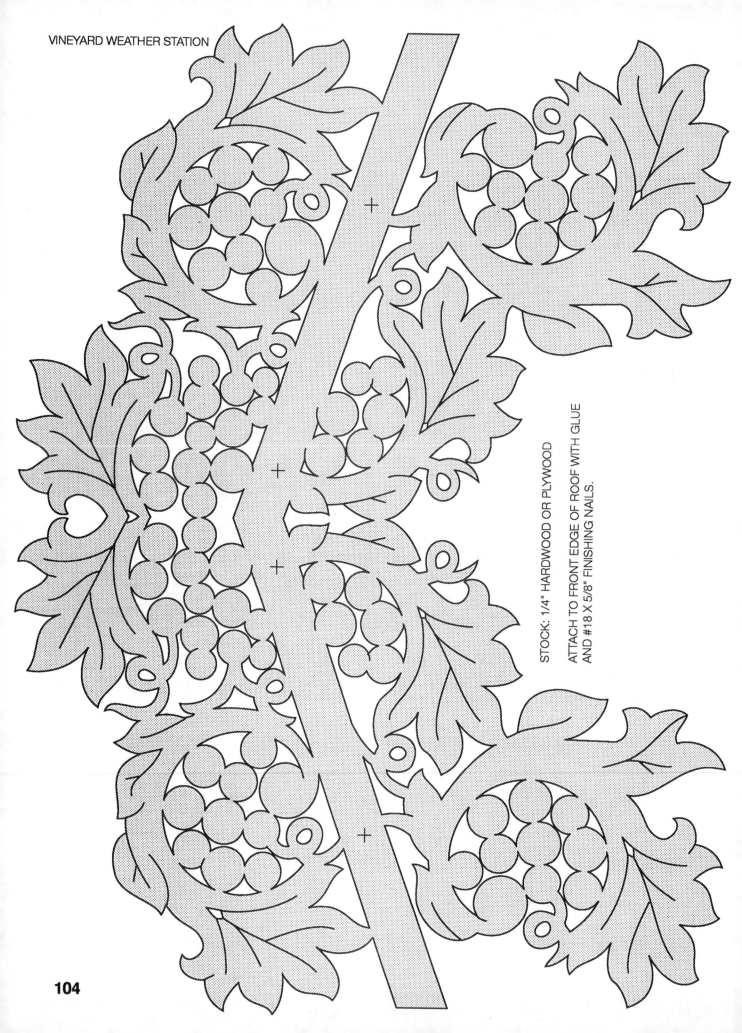

STOCK: 1/4" HARDWOOD OR PLYWOOD

ATTACH TO FRONT EDGE OF ROOF WITH GLUE
AND #18 X 5/8" FINISHING NAILS.

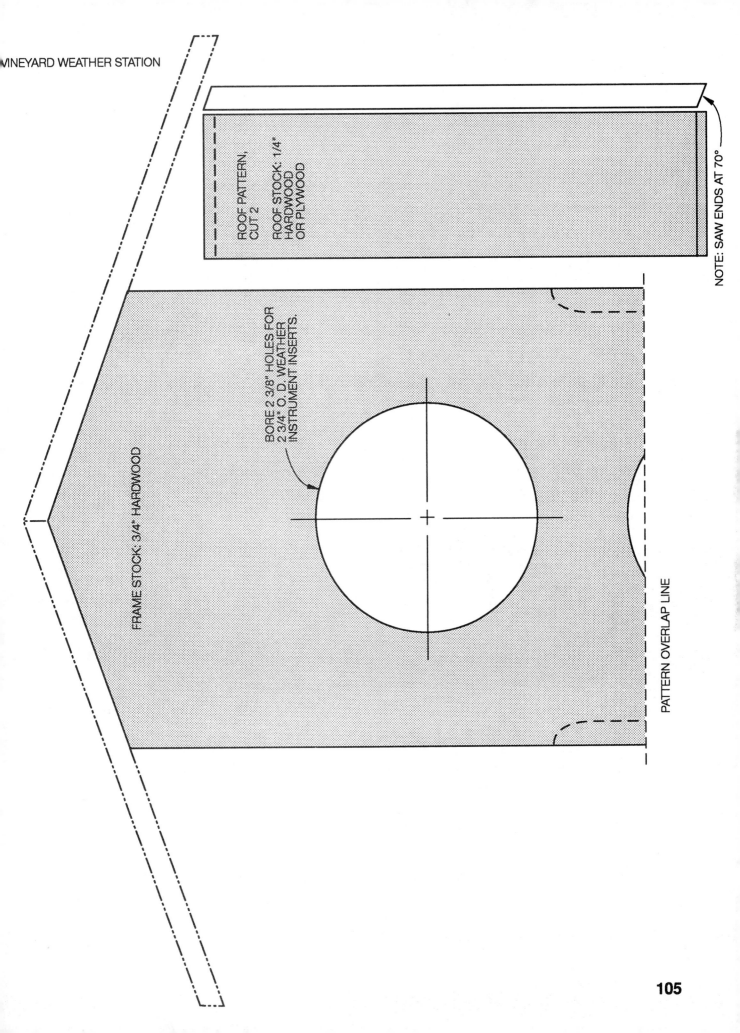

ROOF PATTERN, CUT 2

ROOF STOCK: 1/4" HARDWOOD OR PLYWOOD

NOTE: SAW ENDS AT 70°

BORE 2 3/8" HOLES FOR 2 3/4" O. D. WEATHER INSTRUMENT INSERTS.

FRAME STOCK: 3/4" HARDWOOD

PATTERN OVERLAP LINE

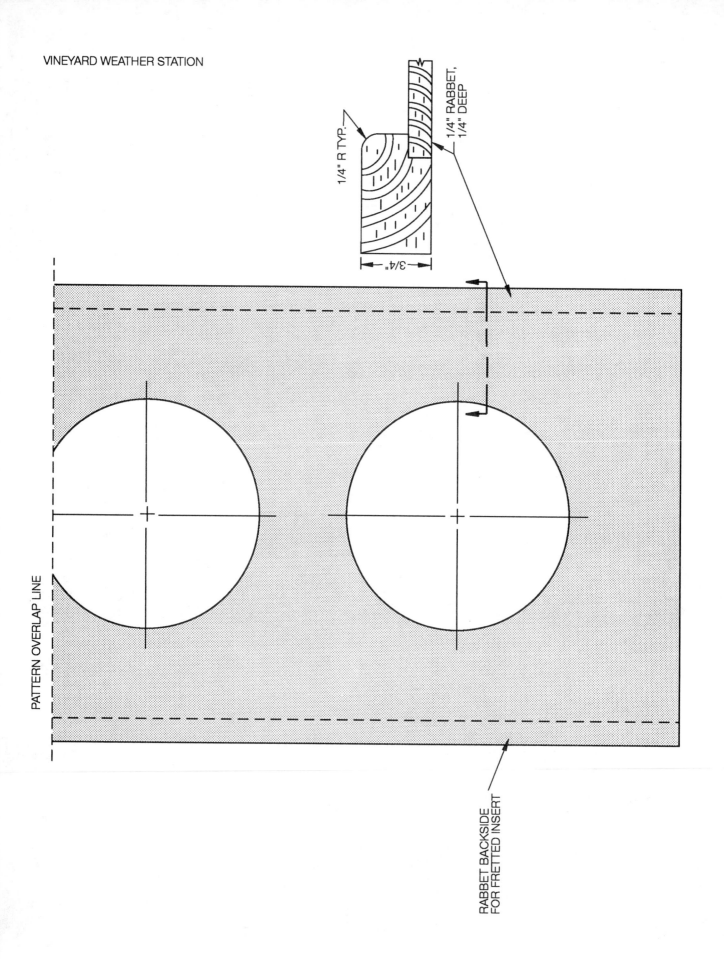

1/4" R TYP.

1/4" RABBET, 1/4" DEEP

←—3/4"—→

PATTERN OVERLAP LINE

RABBET BACKSIDE FOR FRETTED INSERT

VINEYARD WEATHER STATION

SIDE INSERT STOCK: 1/4" HARDWOOD
OR PLYWOOD. CUT 2

ATTACH TO BACKSIDE OF
3/4" FRAME STOCK WITH
GLUE AND #18 X 5/8"
FINISHING NAILS

ATTACH TO BASE WITH GLUE
AND #18 X 5/8" FINISHING NAILS.

VINEYARD WEATHER STATION

BASE STOCK: 3/4" HARDWOOD

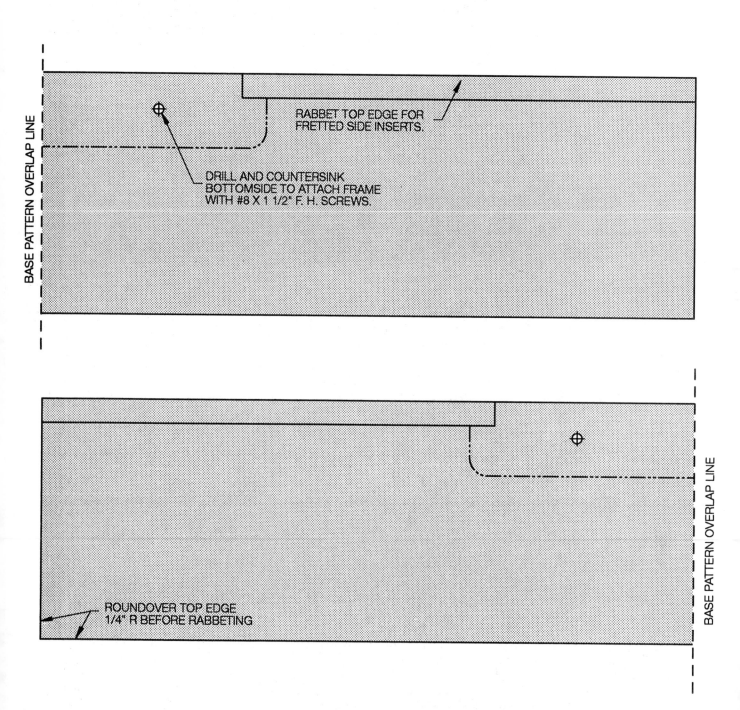

BASE PATTERN OVERLAP LINE

RABBET TOP EDGE FOR
FRETTED SIDE INSERTS.

DRILL AND COUNTERSINK
BOTTOMSIDE TO ATTACH FRAME
WITH #8 X 1 1/2" F. H. SCREWS.

ROUNDOVER TOP EDGE
1/4" R BEFORE RABBETING

BASE PATTERN OVERLAP LINE

VICTORIAN DISPLAY STAND

STOCK: 1/4" HARDWOOD OR
PLYWOOD

NOTE: ASSEMBLE
ALL PARTS WITH #18 X
5/8" FINISH NAILS &
GLUE.

PATTERN OVERLAP LINE

109

PATTERN OVERLAP LINE (VERTICLE)

PATTERN OVERLAP LINE

STOCK: 1/4" HARDWOOD OR PLYWOOD

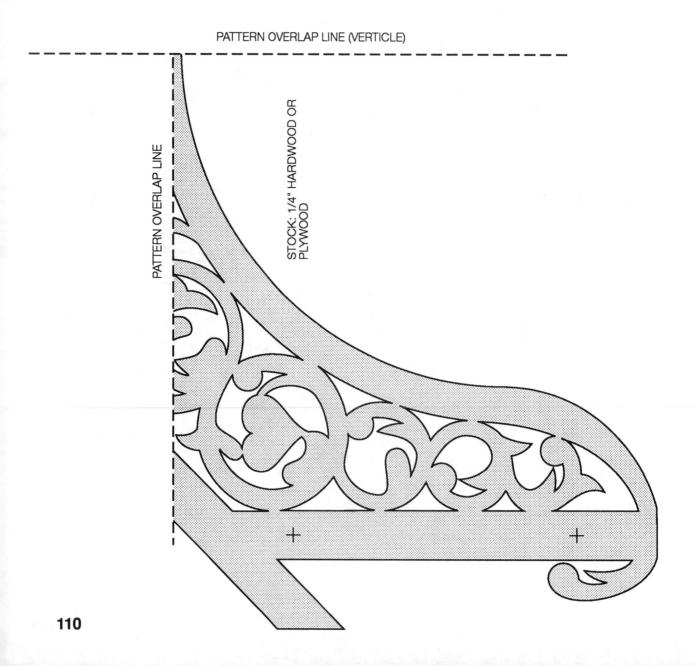

VICTORIAN DISPLAY STAND

STOCK: 1/4" HARDWOOD
OR PLYWOOD

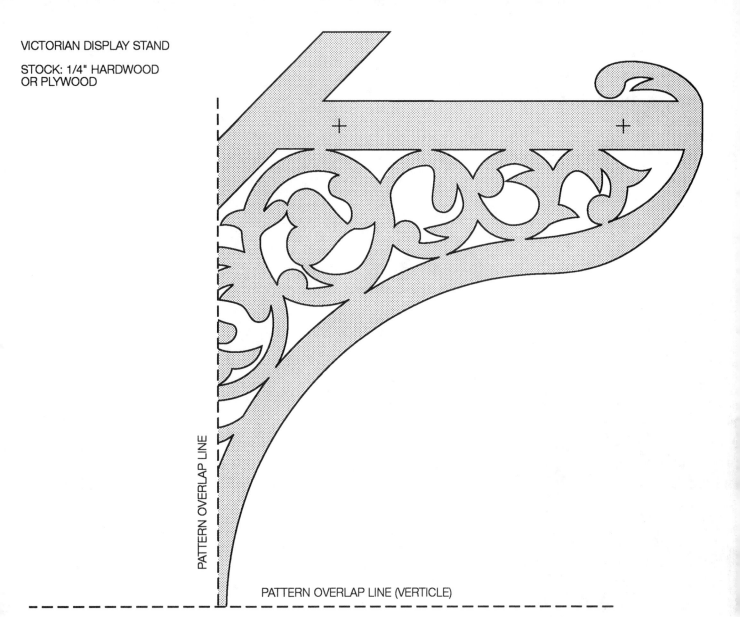

PATTERN OVERLAP LINE

PATTERN OVERLAP LINE (VERTICLE)

VICTORIAN DISPLAY STAND

BACK STOCK: 1/4" HARDWOOD OR PLYWOOD

GLUE AND NAIL TO BOTTOM

BACK PATTERN OVERLAP LINE

BACK PATTERN OVERLAP LINE

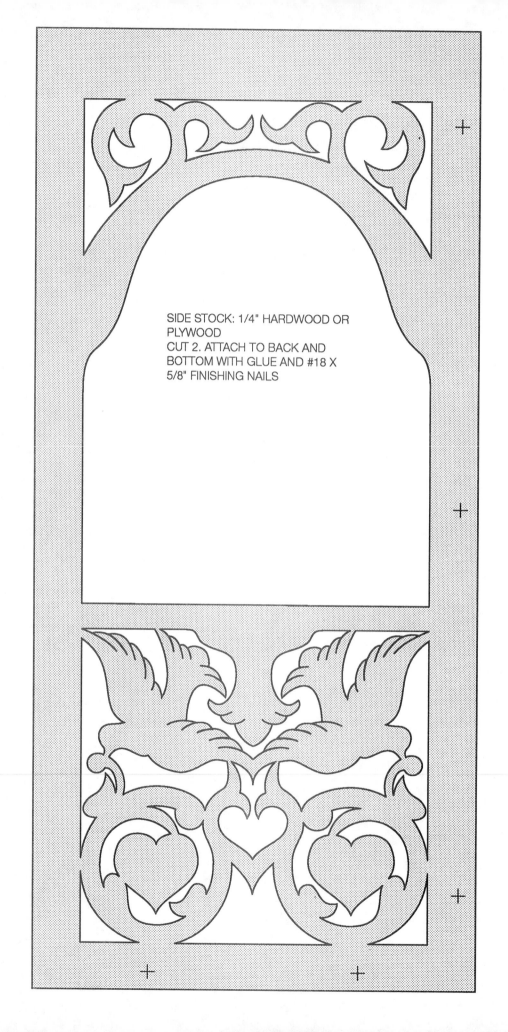

SIDE STOCK: 1/4" HARDWOOD OR
PLYWOOD
CUT 2. ATTACH TO BACK AND
BOTTOM WITH GLUE AND #18 X
5/8" FINISHING NAILS

VICTORIAN DISPLAY STAND

ROOF STOCK: 1/4" HARDWOOD OR PLYWOOD
CUT 2. GLUE AND NAIL TO BACK

NOTE: SAW ENDS AT 45°

ROOF, EDGE VIEW

NOTE: SAW ENDS AT 45°

VICTORIAN DISPLAY STAND

BOTTOM STOCK: 1/4"
HARDWOOD OR PLYWOOD

CENTER BOTTOM ON BASE FROM
SIDE TO SIDE AND 1/4" FROM THE
BACK OF THE BASE. GLUE AND
NAIL INTO POSITION.

ROUNDOVER 1/4" R

VICTORIAN DISPLAY STAND

BASE STOCK: 1/4" HARDWOOD OR PLYWOOD

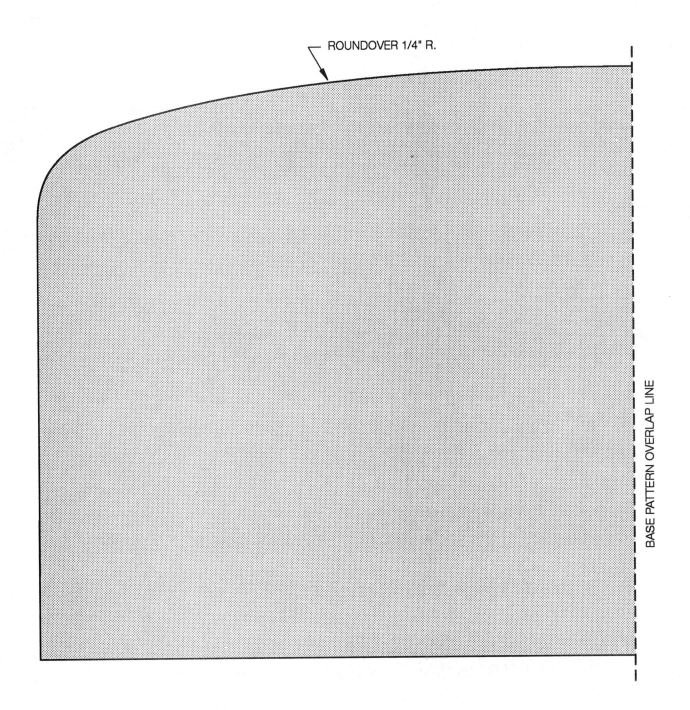

ROUNDOVER 1/4" R.

BASE PATTERN OVERLAP LINE

BASE PATTERN OVERLAP LINE

VICTORIAN CLOCK

STOCK: 3/8" HARDWOOD OR PLYWOOD

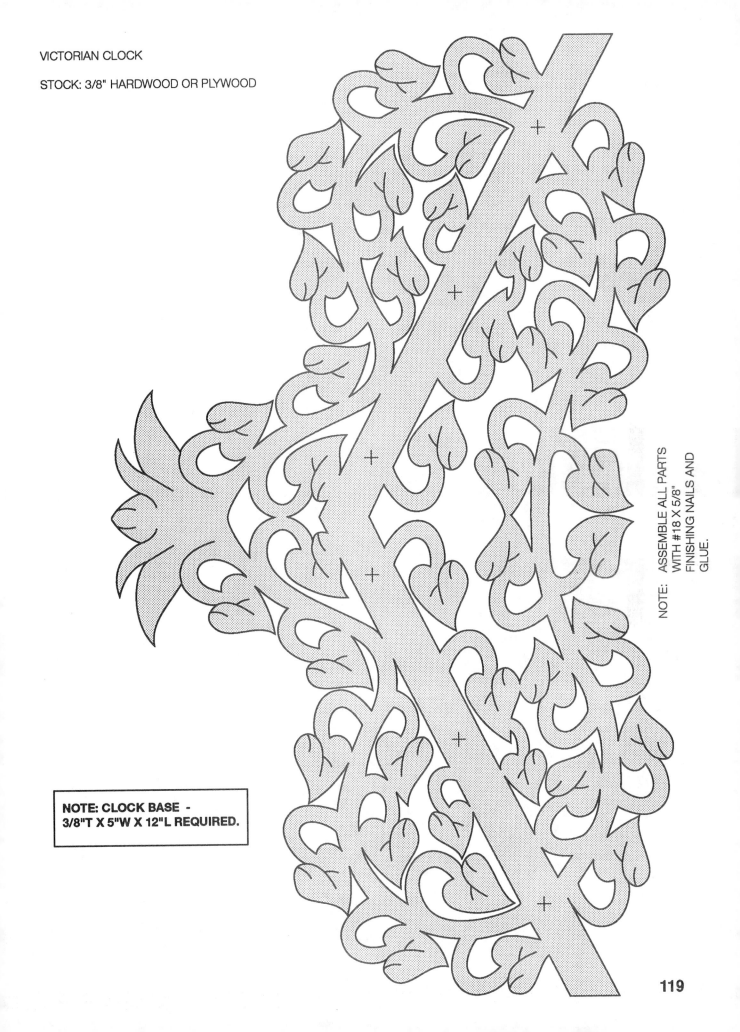

NOTE: CLOCK BASE -
3/8"T X 5"W X 12"L REQUIRED.

NOTE: ASSEMBLE ALL PARTS WITH #18 X 5/8" FINISHING NAILS AND GLUE.

VICTORIAN CLOCK

STOCK: 3/8" HARDWOOD
OR PLYWOOD

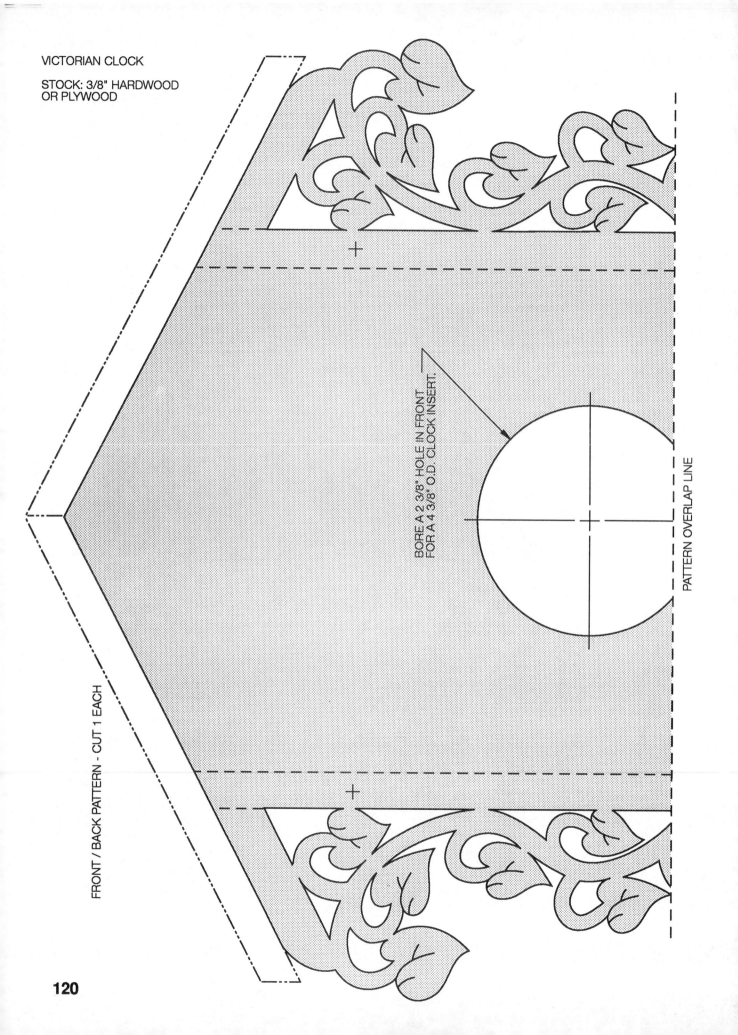

BORE A 2 3/8" HOLE IN FRONT
FOR A 4 3/8" O.D CLOCK INSERT.

PATTERN OVERLAP LINE

FRONT / BACK PATTERN - CUT 1 EACH

PATTERN OVERLAP LINE

NOTE: A CLOCK BASE IS REQUIRED 3/8"T X 5"W X 12"L.

FOR EASE OF ASSEMBLY CUT A
BLANK 3/8"T X 3 1/4"W X 5 1/4"L.
CENTER THIS PIECE ON THE BASE
FROM SIDE TO SIDE AND 3/8" FROM
THE BACK OF THE BASE. GLUE AND
NAIL INTO POSITION. ASSEMBLE ALL
COMPONENTS, EXCEPT FOR THE
FRONT AND END RAILS, AND SLIP
THIS FRAME OVER THE BLANK.
NAILED TO THE BASE. GLUE AND NAIL
IN PLACE TO THE BLANK. THEN
ATTACH THE RAILS TO THE BASE.

NOTE: ASSEMBLE ALL PARTS WITH #18 X 5/8"
FINISHING NAILS AND GLUE.

VICTORIAN CLOCK

STOCK: 3/8" HARDWOOD
OR PLYWOOD

PATTERN OVERLAP LINE

GLUE AND NAIL TO BLANK
ON TOP OF BASE WITH
#18 X 5/8" FINISHING NAILS.

BEVEL TOP 28°

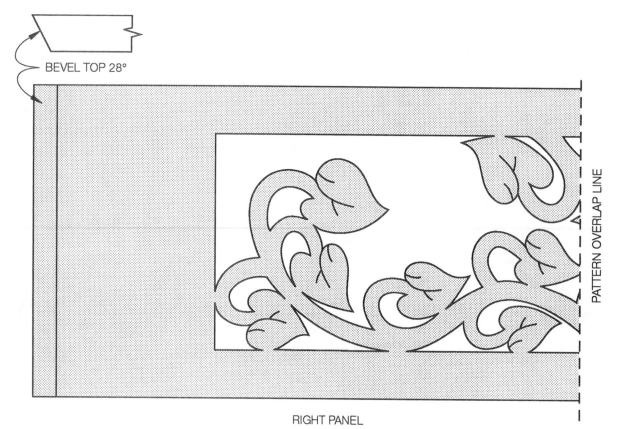

PATTERN OVERLAP LINE

RIGHT PANEL

VICTORIAN CLOCK

STOCK 3/8" HARDWOOD
OR PLYWOOD

PATTERN OVERLAP LINE

GLUE AND NAIL TO BLANK
ON TOP OF BASE WITH
#18 X 5/8" FINISHING NAILS.

BEVEL TOP 28°

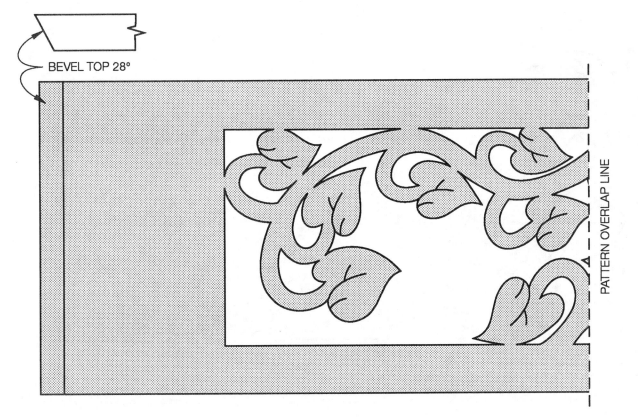

PATTERN OVERLAP LINE

LEFT PANEL

PATTERN OVERLAP LINE

FRONT RAIL STOCK: 3/8"
HARDWOOD OR PLYWOOD.
GLUE AND NAIL TO BASE.

PATTERN OVERLAP LINE

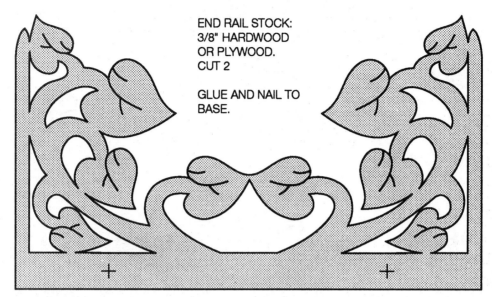

END RAIL STOCK:
3/8" HARDWOOD
OR PLYWOOD.
CUT 2

GLUE AND NAIL TO
BASE.

NOTE: BEVEL 28°   NOTE: BEVEL 28°

ROOF, EDGE VIEW

ROOF STOCK: 3/8" HARDWOOD OR
PLYWOOD.
CUT 2

Product Sources

CLOCKS

The Berry Basket
PO Box 925-BK3
Centralia, WA 98531
1-800-206-9009

Klockit
PO Box 636
Lake Geneva, WI 53147

Precision Movement
PO Box 689
Emmaus, PA 18049

Turncraft Clocks
PO Box 100
Mound, MN 55364

MIRRORS

The Berry Basket
PO Box 925-BK3
Centralia, WA 98531
1-800-206-9009

Woodworker's Supply
1108 N Glenn Rd
Casper, WY 82601

LUMBER

Constantine's
2050 Eastchester Rd
Bronx, NY 10461

Craftsman Wood Service
1735 West Cortland Ct.
Addison, IL 60101

Good Hope Hardwoods
1627 New London Rd
Landernberg, PA 19350

Sandy Pond Hardwoods
921-A Lancaster Pike
Quarryville, PA 17566

Woodcraft
PO Box 1686
Parkersburg, WV 26102

FREE CATALOG OFFER

Are you interested in more unique designs?

Yes, please add my name to your mailing list for a catalog of more unique ideas.

NAME _____

ADDRESS _____

CITY _____ STATE _____ ZIP_____

THE BERRY BASKET PO BOX 925-BK3 • CENTRALIA, WA 98531 • 1-800-206-9009

Do you have friends who are interested in a catalog of unique ideas?

Yes, please add my friend to your mailing list and send them a catalog of unique ideas.

NAME _____

ADDRESS _____

CITY _____ STATE _____ ZIP_____

THE BERRY BASKET PO BOX 925-BK3 • CENTRALIA, WA 98531 • 1-800-206-9009

WOODWORKING SURVEY

We always appreciate when people take time to write and let us know what they like and what they'd like to see more of. We know more of you would like to do the same, but find it hard to find the time. So here's an opportunity to do just that! It's easy - just grab a pen and mark a box! We'll personally look at every survey returned and use your responses to help design future patterns and projects.

1. My skill level is:

☐ Beginner ☐ Intermediate ☐ Advanced

2. I like to complete projects that are:

☐ Simple ☐ Intermediate ☐ Intricate

3. I prefer projects that require:

☐ Thin material ☐ Thick material (3/4" or more)

☐ Both

4. I feel the amount of instructions/directions pertaining to the patterns/projects in this book are:

☐ Clear and sufficient

☐ Unclear and incomplete

5. My favorite pattern themes are: (mark all that apply)

☐ Wildlife ☐ Religious

☐ Country ☐ Floral

☐ Victorian ☐ Sports

☐ Southwest ☐ Holiday/Celebration

☐ Children's ☐ Other _____

6. I would like more of the following projects:

(mark all that apply)

☐ Clocks ☐ Baskets

☐ Shelves ☐ Mirrors/Picture Frames

☐ Doll Furniture ☐ Plaques

☐ Birdhouses ☐ Other_____

Fold here second

- -

The Berry Basket
PO Box 925-BK3
Centralia, WA 98531

The Berry Basket
PO Box 925-BK3
Centralia, WA 98531

- -

Fold here first